CONCILIUM

Editorial: Christianity – A Multi-cultural Experiment

N. Greinacher and N. Mette

The young Christian community in Corinth was unimaginably varied. Like the population of the city generally, it too was made up of people of very different cultural and religious origins and background. Nowadays this community would be called 'multicultural', and as such it was no exception within a church which already at that time had a multicultural stamp (e.g. Antioch).

However, the fact that once the conflict over circumcision had been resolved, Christianity was thus manifestly open to all cultures, does not mean that it simply assimilated to them. At the heart of Christian belief stand notions and practices which are diametrically opposed to the customs of its contemporary environment (e.g. Gal. 3.28). Hence conversion to this faith involved a renunciation of the dominant culture where it ran counter to the principles of faith. At the same time, however, this did not amount to an encapsulation: Christians were firmly convinced that their faith not only led to personal salvation but also had a decisive contribution to make to the shaping of a social life that was pleasing to God.

With its readiness for multicultural encounters and experiences, Christianity is in continuity with the centuries of Israelite tradition. So it is all the more tragic that not least on this point there was a demarcation which finally led to a split. This had a disastrous effect above all because the ongoing expansion of Christianity and its successful assimilation to the Graeco-Roman spirit led to a sense of cultural superiority which produced an increasingly exclusive and irreconcilable attitude towards other cultures – first of all to Judaism. It was largely forgotten that Christianity had begun as what Johann Baptist Metz has called a 'multicultural experiment'.

In the meantime, the self-critical objection has been made that what has sometimes euphemistically been called 'cultural encounter' has in fact meant the destruction of the old in favour of a monopoly of 'Christian' culture. However, it is surely more in keeping with the nature of Christian faith that people have become aware of the need for its 'inculturation' and that many efforts have been made in this direction (also leading to the discovery that this is far from being a totally new enterprise). Nevertheless, by no means all questions and problems have been solved. On the contrary, many are emerging again with renewed force. For example, is Christianity in principle culture-neutral, and can it therefore be assimilated to any culture? Or are there also cultural achievements to which Christianity has contributed in the course of history, and on which it should not go back? If so, what are these achievements? And where may perhaps objections and contradictions be made in the light of the gospel to particular elements of culture which are taken for granted? And in turn, what does that mean for the process – or better, processes – of inculturation?

This is not the first time that these and further questions have been taken up and discussed in *Concilium*. But there are two reasons for returning to them now. First, after a debate on inculturation within theology and the church which has now lasted thirty years,[1] some problems have come to be seen more clearly. Secondly, 'inculturation' is threatening to degenerate into a term which can be exploited by the most varied interests in church politics. So it is time to put this topic on the agenda once again. The aim of this issue is to deal with it partly in principle, and partly by way of examples. At the heart of the discussion lies the question of which experiences and impulses towards action – in the twofold sense of a disclosure of new dimensions of the gospel through the other culture and a critique of the gospel by it – arise from an inculturation which is more than mere accommodation, for Christian faith and Christian life on the one hand and a particular culture on the other.

The section 'Fundamental Aspects' begins with a contribution from biblical theology. Silvia Schroer selects examples to demonstrate that the Bible is a document of intercultural learning and shows how it has this character. Israel's identity had to be established in constant controversy with the surrounding cultures and religions and was also constantly reshaped by them. One particularly clear symbol of this intercultural and interreligious dialogue is Sophia in the book of Wisdom, in which the encounter between the Jewish and Hellenistic Greek wisdom tradition is expressed by means of a personification. It emerges that Israel's own cultural and religious identity is enormously enriched, and can also illuminate the other culture by being interpreted anew in the light of an alien tradition. However, such changes in the Jewish wisdom tradition need to be measured by the question whether they serve the righteousness of God – which must be put into practice.

For some time there has been an argument in church and theology over two models of inculturation: whereas one stresses the transcendence of the gospel over any culture, so that it can be introduced into any culture as an independent entity, conversely the other stresses the dynamic of the culture in which even the gospel is inevitably involved. According to Robert Schreiter, while there are true insights in both models, in the last resort they result in an aporia. So in his view it is important to clarify in advance what is understood by faith and what by culture. From this clarification different possible relationships result, which are not necessarily mutually exclusive, but are to be seen as standing in dialectical tension with each other.

Giancarlo Collet attacks exaggerated and indeed sometimes euphoric expectations which can often be encountered in connection with program-matic talk of the 'inculturation of Christianity'. He warns us that not least the ambivalent experiences of multiculturalism and the way in which the social and political challenges associated with it are dealt with calls for sober realism. This also applies to the sphere of the church. Despite all the solemn formulas, it often remains unclear what precisely is meant by 'inculturation'. According to Collet, the only way forward is to focus on the subjects of the evangelization and take them seriously, above all the local churches and the communities (including base communities) of Christians who attempt to face the promise and challenge of the gospel in their concrete context. Where that really happens, inculturation comes about as it were incidentally, without the need to direct every possible effort towards it.

There follow five *case studies* of experiences of Christianity in various cultures, past and present. Maurice Assad describes the way taken by Coptic Christianity in Egypt from its beginnings to the present day and shows how this way was and is directed by a constant concern to maintain its own identity through cultural change while at the same time taking note of the new challenges which arise. F. Kabasele Lumbala shows in the case of his home country, Zaire, the degree to which a Christianity with a colonial stamp led to its alienation from cultural traditions and people there, and also what an enrichment for Christian faith generally a real inculturation there could be. Mariam Francis writes about the difficult situation of the churches and their members as a minority in Pakistan, since the laws of this country exclusively favour Islam and exclude all other religions from politics, etc. She sees the specific contribution of Christians in her cultural context as being to break through the unjust caste system and to contribute to a gradual change in the prevalent discriminatory attitudes and practices by an unswerving call for a humane society. Fernando Castillo makes a critical reconstruction, in connection with Latin America, of the problems posed for a Christianity which attempts to play a role in creating and shaping culture. He resolutely opposes the notion of a 'Christian culture', which has emerged again in church discussion, and sees the test of Christian faith as being whether it becomes inculturated among the victims of the process of modernization, the impoverished and the excluded, and takes their side. Finally, Jean-Guy Nadeau demonstrates by means of the youth cultures in Canada the abysmal alienation between traditional Christianity and society which has come about in the process of social modernization. Despite all the problems, he also sees a possibility here for both youth and the church to encounter the gospel anew. At the same time this contribution makes it clear that the question of inculturation is by no means just a concern for the traditional 'mission countries'.

Three contributions go into *select questions in the current discussion*. Gregory Baum sets some question marks against the debate on inculturation and multiculturalism which is being carried on all over the world. He shows how problems are caused by the tendency of some accepted views and approaches which are dominant in the truest sense of the word simply to subsume minorities. In a provocative article, Paulo Suess makes a critical evaluation of the experiences of the Fourth General Assembly of the Latin American episcopate in Santo Domingo in 1992. In the light of the world-weariness and hard-heartedness of a considerable number of bishops as experienced at this conference, he asks how serious they really are about the inculturation to which they so often appeal. Has not this term often come to be used as a slogan under which the baneful traditional concern to dominate continues to wield the real influence? As Vatican II began to show in a pioneering way, the church is called on to reflect fundamentally on its mission of hope in the context of the social developments which are taking place all over the world. It must take the side of the excluded, and from there give new expression to the 'character of the gospel which lies outside the system and the imperative of the gospel which opposes the system'. Finally, Thomas Groome, starting from the theological axiom that inculturation has ultimately to do with the preparation of the advent of the kingdom of God and thus has this as its decisive criterion, formulates five steps or elements for a pastoral praxis of inculturation in the sense of an intercultural conversation.

Notes

1. Cf. the informative survey by L. J. Custodio, 'Understanding Culture', *Philippiniana Sacra* 27, 1992, no. 80, 279–92.

I · Fundamental Aspects

Transformations of Faith. Documents of Intercultural Learning in the Bible

Silvia Schroer

For years the topic of inculturation has been the focus of specialist theological discussions. It is not only missionary societies which feel challenged to make concrete decisions about how the Christian message can be proclaimed and lived out in the various cultures. European Christians cannot avoid coming to grips with the Eurocentrism of Christian history, culture and even biblical interpretation in connection with this topic, since it is very often a matter of 'detaching Christianity from European culture and inserting it into another culture'.[1]

The term 'syncretism' often appears in connection with the term 'inculturation', almost as its shadow.[2] In the context of problems relating to inculturation it often functions as an opposite pole, even a bogeyman. It denotes the point at which the identity of Christianity is (allegedly) surrendered or lost in the process of assimilation. However, Christian churches and theologians all over the world are evidently a long way from achieving an open discussion or even a consensus about how the terms syncretistic and syncretism are to be defined. Who would dare to define what is essential and indispensable in a system of religious symbols? Who would make statements on the authenticity of religion or cultic practice?[3] In recent discussion I am most convinced by the position of Andreas Feldtkeller, who in principle disputes the possibility of an objective use of the term 'syncretism' and argues that instead we should speak of a dispute over the limits of systems, in which all those involved violate the need which other participants have to draw lines, thus endangering their identities.[4]

In a situation of uncertainties, obscurities and identity crisis of the kind that the way of inculturation always represents, it is particularly important to look back in history to the origins of our faith. For both the faith of Israel and the faith of the first Christian generarions arose through processes of inculturation and went through some 'syncretism'. The Bible, the message of which is today translated into the cultures of Asia, Latin America and Africa, is itself a document of intercultural learning and a quest for identity from the time of its origin. Finally, on the way to Europe this document had to be inculturated for us, too, in a tremendous missionary effort.

As an Old Testament scholar, in what follows I shall limit myself to examples from the pre-Christian period. Of course early Christianity offers just as fertile a field of research for the topic, and one which, particularly recently, has been cultivated intensively.[5]

I. Israel – a people in the midst of ancient Near Eastern cultures

The statement that the tiny land of Palestine and its population were part of the Near East may at first sight seem a truism. But the effects of dialectical theology, which put so much stress on the special character of Israel and the verticality of revelation, make it necessary to keep pointing out how Israel was bound up in the great cultural areas of the time. The biblical texts document it at every stage, whether over anthropology or pictures of the world, the image of the king or the image of God, the origin of mythical narrative material or the genres and contents of love songs, collections of instructions for living or proverbs, or legal corpora. Even a glance at the specialist literature will show that there is little that was not influenced in a complex way by Ugarit, Egypt, Syria, Assyria or Babylonia. This interweaving is of course attested not only by the texts but also by the material culture, and above all by the motifs of pictorial art from Palestine.[6]

The relationship between Israel and Canaan is a special instance of the relationship between Israel and its neighbouring cultures. From a historical perspective these two entities were very closely connected. The greater part of the Israelite population had always lived in the land and was therefore of Canaanite origin, speaking the language of that country (cf. Ezek. 16.3; Gen. 10.15f.; Isa. 19.18), though its way of life and culture must have been more markedly agricultural (keeping flocks and tilling the land) than urban. Over centuries the identity of Israel took shape in a vigorous struggle with and demarcation from the culture and religion of Canaan. The narratives about the patriarchs and the Exodus stress that Israel came from outside Canaan. Above all Hosea and, following him,

Deuteronomy, which came into being in the seventh century, did not weary of emphasizing the corruption of Canaan and the difference between Israel and other peoples. Baal became the symbol for a dissolute life and idolatry. Controversies which are really domestic to Israel, e.g. over sexual morality, child sacrifice, the veneration of sacred stones and trees, the star cult and soothsaying practices, are projected on to 'Canaan'.

II. Psalm 65: testimony to an integrative Yahweh faith

In view of this hostile relationship it is all the more amazing that the First Testament has also preserved the gentle voices of the YHWH adherents who got little from the polemic against Canaan and separation from it, and instead attempted to integrate the legacy of Canaan into their religion in a positive way; indeed they were able to carry on an intercultural and interreligious dialogue with it. Psalm 65 is unobtrusive testimony to such groups; so far little attention has been paid to it:[7]

1. To the choirmaster. A Psalm of David. A Song

2a Praise 'is due' to you,
2b God on Zion,
2c and to you people perform vows.
3a You hear prayer.
3b To you all flesh 'brings'
4a accounts of sin.
4b If our transgressions become too great for us,
4c you forgive them.
5a.Happy is the one whom you choose and allow to approach,
5b to dwell in your courts.
5c We shall be satisfied with the goodness of your house,
5d holy is your temple.

6a With dread deeds you respond to us in righteousness,
6b O God of our salvation,
6c the confidence of all the distant
6d ends of the earth and the sea.
7a By your strength you establish the mountains,
7b and gird them with your power,
8a you still the raging of the sea,
8b the roaring of its waves,
8c the tumult of the nations,
9a so that the inhabitants of the ends of the world are afraid
9b at your signs.
10a You visit the earth and pour water upon it,

10b and make it abundantly fertile.
10c The river of God is full of water.
10d You prepare 'their' grain,
10e indeed, you prepare it,
11a watering its furrows, 'levelling' its 'ridges',
11b you soften it with showers of rain and bless its growth.
12a You have crowned the year with your goodness,
12b and your tracks drip with fat.
13a The pastures of the wilderness drip,
13b the hills gird themselves with joy,
14a the meadows clothe themselves with herds,
14b the valleys deck themselves with grain,
15b they shout and sing together for joy.

This psalm is dedicated to God on Zion and the cult in the Jerusalem temple (vv. 2–5). In the second part, in the classical themes of ancient Near Eastern and Israelite wisdom it sings the praise of the creator God who has the threatening powers of chaos under control (vv. 6–9). In the third part, the scene of the divine activity changes yet again. Verses 10–15 are a hymn to YHWH who brings rain and guarantees fertility, is concerned to water the earth and make the seed and the flocks flourish. The image of YHWH which appears in these verses corresponds quite clearly to the image of the great storm- and rain-god Baal. A brief rain hymn from the Keret epic (KTU 1,16, III 1–10) is a particularly good indication of the affinity, since here quite similar motives appear to those in Ps. 65, though this does not mean that we must assume literary dependence:

He poured oil (of salvation into the cup).
The stream 'darkened' earth and heaven.
It went to the ends of the earth,
for the wheat the stream is the source,
for the earth the rain of Baal,
for the field the rain of the Most High.
The rain of Baal is a blessing for the earth,
and the rain of the Most High for the field.
There is a blessing for the wheat in the stream.
In the tilling of the field it is like a fragrance,
on the heights like a perfume.
Those who work in the fields raise their heads,
those who grow the corn raise (their heads) in the air.
The bread had (gone out) in the baskets
the wine in the (jars)
to the house of Keret (they went).

The testimony of Psalm 65 is remarkable to the degree that elsewhere the First Testament had some difficulty in transferring the functions of the rainbringer to YHWH. In I Kings 17f. Elijah has to demonstrate formally that it is YHWH, not Baal, who withholds or sends the rain. Many other texts betray in one way or another how unusual or problematical it was to speak of Israel's God as the one who brings rain (e.g. Jer. 14.22). However, the psalm finds it quite natural to speak of God on Zion as the one who fights against chaos and brings rain, i.e. to connect the cult in Jerusalem with the old religious language of the population of the land, the farmers and herders of small cattle, in a tremendously wide theological span. There are even indications that the redactors have as it were put the old Canaanite hymn in vv. 10–14 in the mouth of the 'inhabitants of the ends of the earth', by introducing direct speech after v. 9d and providing a framework for these words of the inhabitants of the ends of the earth by shifting v. 14c to its present place. It is the peoples of the end of the earth who praise Baal with the hymn, but now celebrate YHWH. By this brilliant way of doing theology with quotations, Israel identifies itself with the language and conceptions of Canaan.

Psalm 65 is an encouraging example of the amount of intercultural and interreligious learning which is possible even in difficult circumstances, and also of how much a mature and really believing theology which trusts in the guidance of God can contribute to such a learning process.

III. The inculturation of Jewish faith in Egypt

It may be objected that the preceding example of Psalm 65 as a biblical document of intercultural learning in Israel has contributed little to the question of real inculturation, because inculturation presupposes a more or less closed religious system of symbols which is then 'translated', whereas in Israel many developments were in train right up to the exile. However, there are good reasons for dating Psalm 65 to the post-exilic period. It is quite conceivable that the authors of this text were reacting in an unpolemical way to other more markedly exclusive monotheistic positions.[8] Furthermore the First Testament bears witness to impressive efforts at inculturation in early Judaism, which attempted to anchor Jewish faith in the Graeco-Roman world. The Septuagint came into being in Alexandria between the third and the first centuries BCE; it did not limit itself to the translation of Hebrew texts, but created texts with new content. In these, theological concepts and ideas emerge which sometimes diverge considerably from the originals.[9] The concern for inculturation is

probably the most important driving force behind the works of the early
Jewish historians, philosophers and poets of the Hellenistic Roman period.
It is no coincidence that the late Wisdom writings in particular (Jesus
Sirach, Koheleth and the Wisdom of Solomon) document similar efforts at
inculturation.[10] The Wisdom schools and Wisdom literature in Israel had
long had a certain international character; the authors were aware of their
links with other cultures and had less anxiety about coming into contact
with them than, say, the Deuteronomistic tradition.

IV. The Book of Wisdom

One writing the significance of which as a witness to inculturation has
hitherto not been taken sufficiently into account is the Wisdom of
Solomon. It was composed in Greek and may have been written by authors
with a Greek education in Alexandria in the last three centuries before the
Common Era.[11] The contemporary background is shaped by the destabil-
ized political situation after the naval battle of Actium (31 BCE). The
situation deteriorated for the Jewish communities in Egypt. There were
many apostates, and calumniations and persecutions within the communities. In 30 BCE Egypt became a Roman province.

Under the impact of these events, which were so significant for world
history, the work attempts to stabilize Jewish identity. The authors raise
the voice of reason, remind rulers of their mortality, and in the picture of
Wisdom and the ideal, wise king (Solomon) present the unconditional
presuppositions for a lasting rule which will satisfy the supreme claims of
intelligence and ethics. In a wide-ranging scheme the Jewish tradition is
newly translated to meet the demands of the time, brought up to date,
and also explained for non-Jews. Therefore for example the work pack-
ages biblical narratives about the history of humankind 'incognito' in
Hellenistic Greek by avoiding any mention of biblical names. Material
from Stoic philosophy has found its way into the middle of the book;
Stoic descriptions of the divine stamp the hymns of praise to Sophia
(7.22–8.1).

The authors of Wisdom take the greatest step towards inculturation by
giving a Jewish answer to the challenge of the Greek Isis cult in Egypt.
With the figure of personified Wisdom, Sophia, they not only give new
significance to a female image of God from the post-exilic period,[12] but at
the same time implicitly proclaim a programme of inculturation.

Wisdom 6–8 in particular is devoted to personified Wisdom. As already
in the early Wisdom books, Sophia is portrayed as a companion and

beloved of the disciple of Wisdom. Her nature is not kept secret in mysteries, but proclaimed openly (6.22–25). As architect or builder of all things she instructs the wise in all the scientific disciplines of Hellenism. The relationship between the ideal wise man (Solomon) and Sophia is described in markedly erotic terminology. The erotic language of these images is not new. But it is amazing that it is also transferred to the relationship between God and Wisdom: in 8.3 Wisdom is described as God's beloved and consort. The marital communion of Sophia with God is an image which explains why she is the one above all who shares in the divine knowledge. Only Wisdom, on the basis of her knowledge of the divine and all things, can be a perfect counsellor of a wise king. In his prayer (ch. 9), Solomon, the patron of wisdom, prays to God for the *paredros* (occupier) of the divine throne (9.4). Historically, both the term *paredros* and the image of the enthroned couple are closely connected with the divine couples of the polytheistic religions of the East and of Greece. The authors of the work are not afraid to use bold imagery when they are describing the various aspects of the divine reality.

The figure of personified Wisdom is already strongly inspired by the images and mythology of the ancient Near Eastern and Egyptian goddess cults in the earlier Wisdom writings. Maat, Hathor, the tree goddesses of Egypt and the Syrian goddess give Sophia her image and her power of fascination. The observation that in Wisdom Sophia is normatively shaped by the figure of Isis and Isis theology in late Ptolemaean and early Roman Egypt was already made here and there during the first half of the twentieth century. Major publications by J. M. Reese, B. L. Mack and J. S. Kloppenborg have contributed to bringing out more clearly the connections between Isis and Sophia.[13]

In the late period of Egypt, the cult of the goddess Isis spread over the Aegean and the western Mediterranean through Greece to Italy. The Isis cult owed its popularity to the unlimited versatility of the 'universal goddess'. Her lifegiving and protective functions, described in myth, as sister-consort of Osiris and mother of Horus, made her the mistress of the mystery of life. Rule over the cosmic and earthly powers and over destiny was attributed to Isis, as she was not subject to the Greek goddess of compelling fate, Heimarmene. The Hellenistic Isis aretalogies praise the goddess as the one who gives the peoples languages, alphabets and sciences. She is the patron of seafaring and trade, bestows rule on kings and validity on law; she helps those who pray to her to gain prosperity and the blessing of children. Isis was worshipped right across almost all groups of the population (with the exception of the military), by men and women, but her cult demonstrably had a particular attraction for women and had probably a positive influence on their social position.

Lists can be made of the similarities between the attributes of Isis and those of Sophia in the book of Wisdom. However, mere comparisons of motifs are of little value when some of the epithets can also be found in hymns to other deities (e.g. Zeus): thus a specific connection with the Isis cult cannot really be demonstrated. Kloppenborg[14] therefore attempts to discover the wider theological conceptions which can be recognized behind the epithets and to connect this theology with Sophia theology. He distinguishes three types of Isis worship in the first century BCE: the Isis worship of ordinary people, that of the Ptolemaic and Roman kingship theology, and that of the Greeks which we find in the aretalogies, in Plutarch or Diodore of Sicily. Whereas the first type had hardly any influence on Alexandrian Judaism, the authors of the book very deliberately come to grips with kingship theology, and above all with the markedly missionary Isis worship of the Greeks.

The extensive description of Solomon and Wisdom in the middle of the book takes on a particular mythological dimension against the background of the Isis-kingship theology. Just as Solomon attains immortality through Wisdom, so Osiris and Horus gain immortality through Isis. Just as Sophia is at the same time 'goddess' and (longed-for) consort of the king, so Isis is goddess and consort of the king, counsellor and guarantor of the ruling house. She ends injustice, tyranny and wars.

In many dedication inscriptions Isis is celebrated as the saviour (of all), as she has power over fate and all the forces of the cosmos. She is the patron of farmers, seafaring people, prisoners, those seeking justice, married couples and mothers, and also scholars. She is believed to be able to save from distress at sea, imprisonment and other disasters, and helps her worshippers to prosperity, knowledge in all spheres, success in their profession and a long life. She is responsible for justice and morality, gives laws, and sees to it that they are kept, so that all people can live as equals in peace. Similarly, above all in Wisdom 10, but also in numerous other passages, there is a description of the saving power of Sophia who can steer a ship (10.4; 14.1–6), come to prisoners in the dungeon (10.14), create riches for the just (3.3–6), and so on.

The statements about Sophia in the book of Wisdom are profoundly steeped in Isis mythology; indeed, they quite deliberately use the language of the Isis mission in quotations and allusions in order to paint a picture of Sophia. Sophia is the Jewish answer to the challenge of the piety of Isis and the mysteries in Egypt just before the beginning of the Common Era. What is worth noting about this answer is that it does not consist in a negative delimitation but in constructive integration. The book of Wisdom is addressed to Jewish men and women, perhaps also sympathizers with Judaism, who came directly into contact with Isis worship, in Alexandria, and for whom the Isis cult could possibly be a quite real religious alternative. Instead of demonizing Isis religion, the work attempts to set a figure of equal status alongside Isis. This attempt reflects, first, a readiness on the part of Judaism in Alexandria to accommodate Greek culture, education and religion and take guidelines from it, though there was an unwillingness to allow certain aspects (e.g. the piety of the mysteries, the worship of idols, the ruler cult, etc.). Secondly, something of women's history takes shape in this theological outline. Both the Egyptian women and the Greek women in Egypt had considerable legal and economic freedom. There was discussion of the traditional roles of women in the philosophical schools. Moreover, a consequence of the Hellenistic emancipation of the individual was that the practice of religion was sometimes taken over by private cultic associations from among which individuals could make a choice. These changes inevitably left a mark on Jewish men and women living in Alexandria. And Jewish women (especially the upper classes) may have formulated claims with increasing self-awareness that they had an active share in the shaping of religious life and could formulate 'modern' approaches to faith capable of offering images of God which could speak to their times.[15]

V. Sophia in the book of Wisdom – a symbol of the unity of cultural multiplicity and a teacher of righteousness

As a personification, Sophia in the Book of Wisdom combines all the Jewish wisdom tradition with the Hellenistic Greek tradition. Thus it mediates between biblical wisdom teaching with its marked ethical orientation and interest in a just order and the intellectual conception of wisdom in Greek antiquity, which in turn joined in the philosophical and ethical quest for the supreme good and the greatest happiness. The message of the work is that what for Hellenists is philo-sophia, a concern for wisdom, can also be found in the Jewish tradition. The striving for knowledge and education is seen as something that the two cultural circles have in common, as the foundation for an inter-cultural dialogue. The religious and national identity of educated Jewish circles in Alexandria also proved strong enough in times of crisis to react in dialogue to the challenges of the Hellenistic world. This reaction also to some degree had a tradition in Egyptian Diaspora Judaism. The Elephantine community had already gone its very distinctive way in a YHWH worship which similarly had been stamped by openness towards the religious influences in the environment, e.g. over the question of a *paredros* to YHWH.

In Sophia, the nationalism and independence of Israel are combined with universalism and a theologically thought-through inculturation. This dialogue is not uncritical. Wisdom, as Jews understand it, is not a private matter, nor is it restricted to the few who are initiated into mysteries. It is the only guarantee for the existence of any rule, since education is indispensable for a just rule. Against the background of the extensive *Pax romana*, wisdom is a symbol which is critical of domination and directed against arbitrariness and tyranny.

Wisdom appears in the image of the wise, omniscient, just and saving woman whose autonomy is at the same time transparent to both Israel's God and the goddess Isis. As an originally Egyptian goddess, in the Hellenistic-Roman world Isis herself was a religious symbol with an exceptional capacity for bringing about unity. In the assumption of Isis mythology and theology by the figure of Sophia, Egyptian Judaism uses a female divine symbol to give its own powers of integration added force.

Furthermore, the significance of personified Sophia in creating unity also manifests itself in the theological structure of the book. The first part begins with the programmatic appeal, 'Love righteousness, you who judge the earth' (1.1). The purpose of this first part of the book is to demonstrate that, contrary to appearances, the righteous have chosen the better and more rewarding way, indeed that God's ordinances will ultimately prevail. The real world with its unjust ordinances and striving for riches is contrasted with a just world, a counter-world, the symbolism of which is very similar to the New Testament notions of a 'kingdom of God' (cf. 10.10,14). This counter-world is at the same time both in existence, because one can live according to its ordinances, and utopian, because complete righteousness is brought about by God only 'then'. But Wisdom is a teacher of righteousness who is accessible to all. Justice and Wisdom are like the outside and inside of a life which is pleasing to God. There cannot be a righteous 'kingdom of God' without Wisdom.

Sophia in the book of Wisdom is the symbol of an interreligious and intercultural dialogue in a multicultural society of the first century BCE. This attempts to take up the existing pluralism of religions and cultures in a positive way by interpreting their own tradition anew, readily opening itself to alien influences and allowing it to be inspired by them. The 'contextual theology' of scripture is not afraid to speak of the God of Israel in a new language and in images which resemble goddesses. Nevertheless, this process of transformation does not lead to the surrender of proven tradition, to the levelling out of the independence of Jewish faith, or to esoteric randomness. A shared history creates identity 'at every time and in every place' (cf. 19.22). The indispensable criterion in all changes is the righteousness of God. There is a good reason why the book of Wisdom is intensively preoccupied with idolatry and blasphemous worship of rulers (Wisdom 11–19).

Perhaps in the insistence of the work on the connection between wisdom and righteousness we also have one of the most important stimuli for present-day discussion of inculturation and syncretism. What is the weight of orthodoxy and the (supposed) purity of doctrines in the light of the message of the kingdom of God? And is there not a more urgent question, indeed one which is unavoidable for survival on this earth? What religious praxis leads to a more just and healthy human society and relationship between human beings and creation, to just relations between men and women, parents and children, and people with skins of different colour, different nationalities and religions?[16]

Translated by John Bowden

Notes

1. U. Berner, 'Synkretismus und Inkulturation', in H. P. Siller (ed.), *Suchbewegungen. Synkretismus — Kulturelle Identität und kirchliches Bekenntnis*, Darmstadt 1991, 130–144: 132.

2. Cf. Siller (ed.), *Suchbewegungen* (n. 1).

3. As a vivid example one might recall the vigorous controversy provoked by the lecture by the Korean professor of theology Chung Hyun Kyung to the Seventh General Assembly of the World Council of Churches in Canberra in 1991.

4. A. Feldtkeller, *Identitätssuche des syrischen Urchristentums. Mission, Inkulturation und Pluralität im ältesten Heidenchristentum*, Novum Testamentum et Orbis Antiquus 25, Fribourg and Göttingen 1993, esp. 116–120: 119.

5. Feldtkeller, ibid., gives an excellent picture of the tense historical controversies over mission, inculturation and pluralism in Syrian Gentile Christianity. His work, which impressively combines historical investigations with systematic reflections, among other things considers the little-noted fact that from the beginning the Christian groups were confronted with 'syncretisms' in their environment. What attitude was to be adopted to people who integrated elements of Christian faith into their own religious practice without becoming converts?

6. Cf. especially O. Keel and C. Uehlinger, *Göttinnen, Götter und Gottessymbole. Neue Erkenntnisse zur Religionsgeschichte Kanaans und Israels aufgrund bislang unerschlossener Quellen*, Quaestiones Disputatae 134, Freiburg im Breisgau 1992.

7. Cf. my longer article, 'Psalm 65 – Zeugnis eines integrativen JHWH-Glaubens?', *Ugarit Forschungen* 22, 1990, 285–301 (my translation of the psalm).

8. The distinction between exclusive-polemical and inclusive-unpolemical monolatry (or monotheism) stems from the ongoing discussion over monotheism in specialist Old Testament circles (cf. the most recent collection edited by M.-T. Wacker and E. Zenger, *Der eine Gott und die Göttin. Gottesvorstellungen des biblischen Israel im Horizont feministischer Theologie*, Quaestiones Disputatae 135, Freiburg im Breisgau 1991.

9. Cf. e.g. M. Küchler, 'Gott und seine Weisheit in der Septuaginta (Ijob 28; Spr 8)', in H.-J. Klauck (ed.), *Monotheismus und Christologie. Zur Gottesfrage im hellenistischen Judentum und im Urchristentum*, Quaestiones Disputatae 135, Freiburg im Breisgau 1992, 118–43, 218–25.

10. Thus around 130 BCE the grandson of Ben Sira in Egypt translated into Greek the work composed by his grandfather around 180 BCE.

11. For what follows cf. H. Engel, 'Was Weisheit ist und wie sie entstand, will ich verkünden', in G. Hentschel and E. Zenger (eds.), *Lehrerin der Gerechtigkeit*, Leipzig 1991, 67–102; D. Georgi, 'Frau Weisheit oder Das Recht auf Freiheit als schöpferische Kraft', in L. Siegele Wenschkewitz (ed.), *Verdrängte Vergangenheit, die uns bedrängt. Feministische Theologie in der Verantwortung für die Geschichte*, Munich 1988, 243–76; see also my extended article 'Book of Wisdom', in E. Schüssler Fiorenza (ed.), *Searching the Scriptures*, Vol. 2, New York and London 1994.

12. Cf. the feminist exegetical approach to this feminine image of God in my 'Die göttliche Weisheit und der nachexilische Monotheismus', in Wacker and Zenger (eds.), *Der eine Gott und die Göttin* (n. 8), 151–82.

13. M. Reese, *Hellenistic Influence on the Book of Wisdom and its Consequences*, Rome 1970; B. L. Mack, *Logos und Sophia. Untersuchungen zur Weisheitstheologie im hellenistischen Judentum*, Göttingen 1973; J. S. Kloppenborg, 'Isis and Sophia in the Book of Wisdom', *HTR* 75, 1982, 57–84.

14. See n. 13.

15. In my commentary on Wisdom (n. 11 above) I have attempted to demonstrate the affinity of Wisdom to the Therapeutae described by Philo in his work *De vita contemplativa*, who were similarly inspired by wisdom and led a monastic life.

16. The Closing Document of the Fourth Assembly of the Catholic Bible Federation in Bogota makes some encouraging statements on the specific topic of inculturation, under the imapct of the urgent demands of pastoral Bible work worldwide. The document can be obtained in various languages from the Catholic Bible Federation in Stuttgart.

Inculturation of Faith or Identification with Culture?

Robert Schreiter

I. The basic issue

As one follows discussions of the process of inculturation in the past number of years, one is struck by a basic issue that surfaces time and time again: in developing a genuinely inculturated faith or in constructing a local theology, how much emphasis should be placed on the dynamic of faith entering into the process, and how much emphasis should be given to the dynamics of culture already in place?

Church documents – beginning with the discussion of culture in Vatican II's *Gaudium et Spes* and continuing with the writings of Paul VI and John Paul II – have stressed the role of faith encountering the culture. In this scenario, the gospel enters the culture and examines it thoroughly: affirming what is good and true and in turn elevating that goodness and truth to an even more exalted level, but also challenging and correcting what is evil and sinful so as to purify the culture. There is also always a reminder that, while the gospel can indeed become inculturated in every human situation, it also transcends every culture. It is not beholden to or circumscribed by any single human culture. Even cultures where the gospel has been known and faith practised for a very long time (as in the case of European cultures) cannot make a proprietary claim on the gospel. This approach affirms the potential of culture and (especially in the addresses of John Paul II) asserts the right to culture, but consistently and insistently emphasizes the sovereign power of the gospel to move freely and autonomously in its transformation of culture in the process of in-culturation of faith. It should be noted that such an emphasis is more than church authority exercising its responsibility to preserve the faith; it is grounded in a consistent theology of revelation that understands God's word as intimately bound up with creation yet always transcending it.

Another approach prefers to emphasize the dynamics of culture as the starting point. It does not deny the transcending character of the gospel or the power of faith to criticize and transform culture. It shares the same theological commitments as the first position. But it questions whether a scenario of the gospel operating over against culture can really bring about the inculturation of faith that is sought. It stresses that the gospel never enters a culture in pure form; it is always already inculturated – embedded in the culture of the evangelizer. This already inculturated faith will emphasize some features of the message and necessarily de-emphasize others. Moreover, imagining the gospel working in such an autonomous manner over against the culture seems to misunderstand the dynamics of how intercultural communication takes place. It assumes that a message communicated by someone from one culture will be received and understood by someone in another culture precisely in the way that its sender intended. There simply is no guarantee of that – in fact, one can almost count on some measure of miscommunication, mainly because the cultural worlds of the sender and receiver of the message are always in some measure different. Even the most carefully crafted modes of evangelization will always fall somewhat short of the mark. There simply is no plain and pure presentation of the gospel.

Moreover, to the extent that the evangelizer is unaware of how the gospel message is embedded in his or her culture, effective communication – and therefore inculturation – will be in some measure defective or incomplete. Consequently, for genuine inculturation to take place, one must begin with the culture to be evangelized, and imagine a more dialectical approach to the relation between gospel and culture in which the presentation of the gospel is gradually disengaged from its previous cultural embeddedness and is allowed to take on new forms consonant with the new cultural setting.

But, counters the first position, does not such an approach lead to too close an identification of the gospel with culture, and thereby run the risk of diluting or even changing the gospel message? By what criteria can we judge whether this new inculturation is a genuine expression of the gospel and not some false rendering of the gospel message? Might not such an approach render the gospel powerless to judge the sin of a setting because of the demands for a close identification of the gospel with culture? Doesn't this approach foster a dangerous syncretism? Examples of close iden- tification ending in a false presentation of the gospel message are easily conjured up: perhaps the 'German Christians' of the Nazi period in 1930s Germany is the most notorious example.

How would one go about mediating between these two positions? Each affirms an important point: the transcendence of the gospel and the complexity of human cultures. And each position acknowledges the validity of the other's concerns. But neither position has been able to answer the objection of the other: just how does the first position assure that its approach to inculturation is not a form of cultural domination? How does it answer the objection that much so-called Christianization has really been a Westernization? And when will the second position articulate criteria that will assure that close identification with culture does not end in a false inculturation of the gospel?

Satisfying answers to these questions cannot be given in the short compass of an article; nor, probably, would several books suffice to accomplish the task. The reasons for this are several. First of all, we still do not understand the inculturation process all that well. Secondly, we are increasingly aware that differing models of the inculturation process can answer the question differently.[1] And thirdly, there are no agreed-upon definitions of either 'faith' or 'culture' in these discussions.

Some reflections will be presented here on how one might go about working through the complexities surrounding these issues. They begin by focussing on operative definitions of both faith and culture, and then move on to examine what kinds of situations may make one position or the other more desirable as an effective means of inculturation. Finally, there will be a brief look at the question of criteria for judging whether an inculturation is a true one.

II. Images of faith, images of culture

The key to mediating the issue of inculturation of faith or identification with culture is how we understand 'faith' – that which is to be inculturated – and 'culture' – the context or situation in which inculturation takes place. How faith is understood affects what we see as needing to be inculturated, what cannot be substantively changed, and what are the limits of change that can be permitted.

The boundaries of what needs to be inculturated are not as easily drawn as might first seem to be the case. One does not want to be too minimalist in this, and the very fact that we hold to a hierarchy of truths rules out an uncritical maximalist position as well. The debates surrounding the *Universal Catechism* point to how difficult it is to circumscribe Christian belief.

Perhaps the greatest danger is to begin with a reified understanding of faith – that faith is a series of propositions that need to be transmitted. Propositional thinking itself is a culture-bound exercise. And while it can help clarify issues within the context of a single culture, it frequently does not travel well across cultures, even within the same historical period. The great christological controversies in the early history of the church give ample evidence of this. Nor does such thinking respect the fact that our language never captures adequately the mystery of God nor what God has done for us in Christ. The rich theological traditions of the church give testimony to the polysemic density of Christian faith.

This does not, of course, mean that nothing can be defined. But taking again the experience of the early church in the christological controversies – which were often controversies about the meaning of words embedded in different cultures – one can imagine a hermeneutic that would be useful for understanding faith as it moves across cultural boundaries.[2] Just as the bishops at the early councils were reluctant to develop formulae for encompassing the faith, so too perhaps we should follow their lead and read our efforts to define the faith by seeing those pronouncements as negative statements, i.e., boundary language about what *cannot* be said. Such an approach can be seen as an effort at once to preserve the *regula fidei* while at the same time not foreclosing the density of meaning that the faith brings to us. Church teaching would thus be seen not so much as exhaustive statements on a particular issue as at once preserving the integrity of the faith and demarcating it from what cannot be said.

For faith not to be seen in a reified manner will require a more complex understanding, embracing symbol, ritual and ethos. Faith has to be seen as being as much a way as a view of life. This more complex understanding is called for not only because of the rich reality of faith itself, but also because communication in multiple ways and by multiple media enhances the possibility of understanding across cultural boundaries.[3]

How we construe faith affects what we expect to see reproduced in the newly inculturated situation. Is it a matter of getting the words right? Or a matter of symbolic enactment? The replication of certain values? A re-presentation of the Christian story? Our sense of what constitutes an acceptable or effective inculturation will have much to say about what we consider to be 'faith'.

Similarly, how culture is construed has a profound effect on the inculturation process. There is no agreed-upon definition of culture, so again how culture is seen makes a difference. If culture is seen as a worldwide system of rules governing behaviour, then faith has to engage itself with that system. If it is seen as a set of values that offer guidelines for making decisions, then faith enters the culture as values to be upheld or virtues to be achieved. Both of these general approaches see culture largely as a cognitive system, and would evoke a similar cognitive structure from faith. These are among the more traditional understandings of culture. More recent theories emphasize action and performance as models for understanding culture. For example, culture is best understood as a conversation, constantly being constructed by those who participate in it. Or culture is a tool kit that we reach into when we have a problem, but we think little about it when things are going smoothly. Or culture is primarily a performance, understood only when it is enacted.[4]

If one takes a more action-oriented or performance-oriented approach to culture, elements of faith as ethos, ritual and praxis play a larger role. Here perhaps the inculturated faith would best be served by narrative theologies which interlace the local community's story with the larger Christian story.

Which theory of culture we choose will best be determined by the kind of situation the culture finds itself to be in at a given time. This will be explored in the following section. Here it is important to see that there are a variety of understandings of what both faith and culture can be, so when trying to mediate the question of the inculturation of faith or the identification with culture, we must be aware not only of how we define faith and culture, but also of how those definitions carry with them implications that shape the direction of the inculturation process.

III. The situation of a culture and the choice of emphasis

It was noted above that the situation a culture finds itself in may have an effect on one's choice of definitions of faith and culture. This observation is prompted by any examination of Christian experience both in the present and in the past: at times, Christians have felt called to challenge radically a culture, whereas at other times they have defended a culture out of Christian principle. What shapes the choices in these circumstances?

One way of sorting through these choices is to see an inculturated theology addressing alternately the need to affirm the identity of the culture and the need to address social change in a culture.[5] Roughly speaking, decisions to identify with a culture cluster around theologies affirming identity, and decisions to challenge culture with faith around the need for social change. This is not, of course, an absolute distinction, but one that can be helpful in seeing not only how or when such decisions are made, but also something of the principles that motivate those decisions.

There are at least three kinds of situations that seem to prompt a decision to identify strongly with the culture. The first is a situation of *cultural reconstruction*. In this situation, a culture has been so damaged by outside cultural forces that a people has to engage in a conscious reconstruction of their culture. This happens when a culture finds itself in the minority against a larger and more powerful culture and is threatened with extinction. An example would be the situation of indigenous cultures in the Americas. In parts of Canada, for example, peoples in the western part of that country have been borrowing rituals from their neighbours to the south in the United States because their own cultural memory has been so depleted by a century of exploitation and genocide. Another kind of example is the reconstruction of African cultures after the experience of colonialism. That African calls for inculturation seek strong identification with the culture grows out of the need to reinstate the dignity of those cultures as worthy vessels of Christian faith. The reconstruction is different from the first example in that the colonial history must also be confronted and negotiated in a way different from historical patterns of extermination.

A second kind of situation is one of *cultural resistance*. This is the case where a culture is threatened by an alien force and needs to take a posture of resistance in order to survive. One of the clearest examples of this type is the church's intense identification with Polish culture over several centuries of occupation by alien forces. Such patterns of resistance create deep bonds of solidarity, because Christian faith is so intricately bound up with preserving a culture's sense of its own identity and humanity. Similar patterns can be seen in the close identification that grows up in resistance to dictatorships, as was the case in the Philippines and in Chile in the 1970s and 1980s.

A third type of situation is one of *cultural solidarity*. This is a situation where the church is a tiny minority in the population and is suspected of being alien to the majority. In these situations Christians are at pains to show their loyalty and do so by a strong affirmation of the culture. Such would be the case for Christians in China who have had to struggle to show how they are truly Chinese yet part of a universal church.

In all of these situations the identity of a culture needs to be attended to. The church, with its understandings of culture since Vatican II, has affirmed again and again a people's right to culture. If one would want to search for a principle behind these identifications with culture, one could suggest that, without a culture having its own integrity and dignity, as well as the participation of its people, there can be no inculturation of the faith.

That is because without these conditions of integrity and participation, the culture that the faith is inculturated into is fundamentally alienating to the people involved and so cannot speak to their hearts and minds. Thus an identification that bespeaks a care for the culture would seem to be an important component for the inculturation process to take place at all.

On the other hand, there are situations when faith seems called to stand over against the culture. The most obvious kind of situation is when injustice is perpetrated and sanctioned by the culture. Here Christian faith must speak out against the injustice. It must resist explanations that injustice and violence are necessary for the integrity of the culture. To be sure, cultures have particular and even peculiar configurations, but long-term violence does not make it a cultural necessity. Moreover, even if these patterns of injustice could be internally justified, cultural boundaries are now porous because of modern communications; therefore such explanations and justifications of injustice will no longer be believed. An example of this kind of injustice is the treatment of women in many parts of the world. More and more it has become apparent that justifications of their subjugation not only now no longer hold, but were probably only believed by men in those cultures in the first place. Racism is another injustice that simply cannot be tolerated.

A second set of situations where Christian faith seems called upon to engage in a more autonomous critique of culture is when a culture faces strong challenges and does not seem to have the inner resources to meet those challenges, either because of the challenge from without or because of disintegration from within. An example of this might be some of the Eastern European countries whose social values were so corroded by forty years of Communism that they find it difficult to marshall the resources for living in a very different kind of world.

Is there an underlying principle in these sets of situations that guide a decision in the direction of a more autonomous role for faith *vis-à-vis* culture? It might be formulated thus: when a culture experiences a profound lack (no resources for a formidable challenge) or refuses to acknowledge a lack (legitimated injustice), then Christian faith must assume a more autonomous role in the inculturation process.

IV. Criteria for evaluating inculturation

The five sets of situations just discussed – three calling for identification with culture and two for a more autonomous critique of culture – are in some measure limit cases; i.e., they represent the extremes of possibility.

What about all the cases in between? How should one mediate identification and critique in those situations? And how should one judge the results of efforts at inculturation?

Although the situations just described are limit cases, they do provide insight into the cases that fall in between. A useful set of cases might be found in the different strategies of the new evangelization in Latin America, Europe and North America. If a culture does not feel itself to be under acute challenge, yet is faced with an evangelization that is largely a jeremiad against it, or hears a call to faith that seems patently unable to understand the complexities of its situation, that kind of evangelization is likely to fail. There can be no critique of culture without a prior identification with that culture. Otherwise the gospel voice is simply experienced as an alien sound unrelated to reality. One could surmise that the failure of Christianity to reach many Asian peoples has come from this inability to identify.

But on the other hand, an identification with culture that does not offer criticism is an empty one. The gospel, after all, is about *metanoia*, about change. Not to be willing to see a culture grow is not to care about that culture. The deepest commitments of Christianity seem to call both for profound identification, modelled on the incarnation, and transformation, modelled on the passion, death and resurrection of Christ.

Can all of this be translated into criteria for evaluation? Attempts have been made to do this, and while there is some convergence, differences in tradition will cause differences in emphasis.[6] One thing seems certain: no single criterion can be adduced that will give a quick and tidy answer to whether or not the results of inculturation are true to the gospel. We need a number of criteria, working in concert, to answer that question. This is based on what was seen above, namely, that construals of faith and of culture evoke different models and different emphases.

Beyond those criteria that have already been articulated elsewhere (such as consistency with Scripture and the subsequent tradition, the resulting practice, the liturgical life, the quality of discipleship, and so on), I shall conclude with a mixture of principles – two theological and one cultural – that may offer some general orientation to answering the question of the truth of inculturation when used in conjunction with other principles.

First of all, the gospel is about *metanoia* – conversion, change. Consequently, if the gospel enters a culture and nothing changes, then there is no effective inculturation. 'Nothing changes' describes a state in which either the gospel never connects with the culture, or it is allowed to be absorbed into the culture.

Secondly, the culture cannot homogenize the gospel. By this is meant that the culture cannot be permitted to choose which parts of the gospel it chooses to hear and which it chooses to ignore. Cultures must deal with the whole gospel, not simply one with which they feel to be comfortable. This is based on the principle that the gospel transcends every culture and cannot be domesticated by any one of them.

Third, inculturation remains subject to the perils and the possibilities of intercultural communication. An important principle here is that any message communicated across culture boundaries risks both the loss and gain of information and intelligibility. Thus, emphases shift, nuances change, things are forgotten, and new insights are gained. The history of the development of theology and doctrine is testimony to this process. Thus inculturation remains a risk, but it is also a necessary one. Without it, faith cannot take root. With it, the possibility of new and deeper insights into the meaning of the mystery of Christ is always present.

V. Conclusion

From what has been said here, it should be clearer why the inculturation of faith and the identification with culture cannot be seen as an either-or proposition. They represent two moments in the inculturation process which, depending on circumstances, require greater or lesser emphasis. Either acting alone will not suffice. Within the process, how faith and how culture are understood is pivotal to ascertaining the nature and level of inculturation that is taking place. And that ascertainment will continue to require multiple criteria to be adjudicated effectively.

Notes

1. For a review of these models, see Stephen B. Bevans, *Models of Contextual Theology*, New York 1992.

2. Alois Grillmeier, *Jesus der Christus im Glauben der Kirche*, Freiburg 1986, II/I, 19, speaks explicitly of the christological controversies as a process of inculturation.

3. Useful here is Clifford Geertz, 'Ethos, World View and the Analysis of Symbols', in *The Interpretation of Cultures*, New York 1973, 126–41.

4. For culture as conversation, see David Tracy, *The Analogical Imagination*, New York and London 1981; for culture as tool kit, see Ann Swidler, 'Culture in Action: Symbols and Strategies', *American Sociological Review* 51, 1986, 273–86; for culture as performance, see Sam Gill, *Native American Religious Action: A Performance Approach to Religion*, Columbia 1987.

5. This is described in greater detail in Robert Schreiter, *Constructing Local Theologies*, New York and London 1985.

6. For a set of criteria from a Catholic perspective, see ibid., 117–21; for a Reformed perspective, see Anton Wessels, *Images of Jesus : How Jesus is Perceived and Portrayed in Non-European Cultures*, Grand Rapids and London 1990, 158–92.

From Theological Vandalism to Theological Romanticism? Questions about a Multicultural Identity of Christianity

Giancarlo Collet

For several months, on my way to work I have been passing a board containing advertisements for washing powder and a new model of car. On it is also written in somewhat clumsy language a text which asks the population, who at present have to cope with the existence of violent xenophobia, to have more respect and understanding for the increasing number of immigrants who have come into the country. It is anonymous, and goes like this:

> Your Christ is Jewish,
> your car is Japanese,
> your pizza is Italian,
> your democracy is Greek,
> your coffee is Brazilian,
> you holiday in Turkey,
> your numbering is Arabic,
> your writing is Latin,
> so is your neighbour a foreigner?

A hundred yards away on a column, a cigarette firm publicizes its products with racist and sexist posters which are renewed at regular intervals. The agency responsible for the advertising usually takes the same line: external marks of people from which their identity can be inferred – like skin colour, dress, etc. – are mocked in a more or less witty way by being put in a quite alien context. So whereas on the one hand there is a request for respect for others and understanding for foreigners, on the other people are subtly devalued.

I. Multiculturalism as reality and challenge

Multiculturalism has become an unmistakable social fact which is hard to ignore. As the graffito on the poster makes clear, multiculturalism means many things. First, one's own collective and personal identity and the features of its history have grown up in a process of selection from different cultures and participate in them, so that we are culturally determined by others. Secondly, though, we allow ourselves to be determined by others by selecting and taking over some of their achievements. Multiculturalism means above all that people who belong to different cultural traditions live together, indeed have to live together, in one and the same society. For in contrast to earlier times, in which workforces were deliberately recruited from abroad because they were needed, or people voluntarily left their homes because they promised themselves a better life elsewhere, today economic, political and religious causes are forcing millions of people to escape and migrate to economically and politically more stable regions. Here the Third World has to bear the greatest burden. These people, but not just these, are particularly confronted with the problem of multicultural life. However, 'aliens' who were brought in yesterday and were looked on favourably because they were needed, cannot be shown the door today, when economic development has to cope with difficulties, because they are proving a burden. And can one so quickly shut the door on people who for whatever reason, whether voluntarily or by compulsion, leave their home and seek asylum elsewhere, without at the same time asking about one's own contribution to their distress?

However, this latter aspect of a multiculturalism necessitated by worldwide migration and flight becomes clear only when the problem of economic and political interdependence is noted, and a society including those of other cultural origins is not seen as a matter of personal preference but is accepted and actually wanted as a social reality. A look at the background and causes of such multiculturalism detaches it from the casual, starry-eyed waffle of globe-trotters and travel-brochures, which literally promise a blue sky, moves it to the level of reality, and also shows some real difficulties associated with multiculturalism. These difficulties concern first of all those who have to live in a different cultural context and who cannot cope with their new conditions without the enormous amount of adaptation (in matters from eating habits and patterns of behaviour to language) that is expected of them. But a capacity to adapt is also required of those who are at home in a particular culture, although such adaptation can be avoided more easily, and it clearly causes considerable trouble even to those who already have their 'multicultural experiences'. It makes a difference whether multiculturalism is something which lasts for a limited period and is one's own choice, or whether it represents a permanent social situation from which one cannot escape. As long as the individual can still choose whether to spend a holiday in the Bahamas or in a Buddhist monastery, to eat Swiss cheese or Mexican avocados for supper, multiculturalism remains above all a matter of money and taste, and certainly also of one's own psychological capacity for exploring the unknown. But if the alien and other which is so fascinating and so prized outside ordinary routine comes nearer, it suddenly loses its attraction and provokes anxiety. At home one does not extend to foreigners the hospitality by which one was still overwhelmed on the previous visit abroad; at home, a cheerful popular festival with its fixed forms in which one may get caught up by chance and which one may enjoy, is pushed aside as excessive fuss. Multiculturalism contains not only the opportunity for mutual learning but at the same time also a great potential for conflict.

Perspectives and judgments change if multiculturalism is seen as an avoidable fact of social existence, in which different and indeed conflicting notions of value are at stake, for which one has to decide against the background of global interdependence and which also have political implications. The 'mere presence of the alien makes it clear to the native population that their way of thinking which is so illuminating and logical, that their ethical and moral criteria which have been regarded as universal, are evidently only provincial, and that foreigners take them over as a matter of course because they are good and normative'.[1] If in addition the presence of aliens is experienced as a physical threat and a real limitation on existing possibilities, attitudes towards them change quickly and can turn into hatred.

As the social events of recent years have made clear, politicians have not succeeded in grasping the problem of multiculturalism as something to be put on the political agenda, nor can we assume that society has already had sufficient experience in multicultural living and the resolution of the conflicts which arise from it. Rather, we have to prepare ourselves for this manifold challenge and learn to deal with it (something that is discussed under the heading of 'intercultural learning'). In other words, a political culture of multiculturalism is called for, given that 'world society, because of economic dependences, the globalism of financial currents and the worldwide functioning of networks of communication, has become one society, in which different elements struggle for their place. For only when those affected by this opposition are members of one and the same society does the global disparity of living conditions, the contrast between riches and poverty, between prosperity and hunger, become a problem of justice.'[2]

Finally, when it is also remembered that according to the Christian self-understanding foreigners are my brothers and sisters, and that in its claim the gospel specifically excludes ethnocentric discrimination, the question of multiculturalism becomes even more explosive. For the challenge to Christian faith and the church is that in the light of its self-understanding it should overcome any discrimination – 'there is no longer Jew nor Greek, slave nor free, man nor woman' (Gal. 3.28) – without destroying previous cultural identities, but remaking them through the offer of a particular history (cf. Acts 4.12). Accordingly, the practice of Christian faith has to respect others in their otherness and at the same time to grant them the right to a home. This practice includes the rejection both of a ghetto-like self-assertion and of a strategic take-over. What is called for, rather, is the free offer of a new society. So the question of the credibility and relevance of Christianity is bound up with that of its renewed capacity for multiculturalism. Here what needs to be discussed is not primarily the *history* of Christianity, with its many ties to different cultural traditions and its capacity or incapacity to encounter other cultural traditions with respect. Rather, the question is how Christianity can and should establish itself under the conditions of present-day multiculturalism. We may ask whether the situation in central Europe is essentially different from others. In the view of a sociologist of religion the one who 'takes the message of Jesus seriously, and this may be enough as a provisional definition of the term "Christian" . . . in any culture, even a so-called Christian culture, ultimately becomes an outsider'.[3]

If the normative aspect comes more into the foreground, multiculturalism becomes more than a mere description of the present social situation. In that case multiculturalism becomes a programmatic term envisaging a future human society made up of very different cultural traditions. In other words, multiculturalism is not only accepted as an inescapable reality, but is affirmed out of inner conviction and chosen as a social model for the future. This means that 'majority and minority live together with equal rights, in mutual respect and toleration for the attitudes and modes of behaviour of others which have been stamped by different cultures'.[4] In that case multiculturalism not only presupposes unconditional reciprocal recognition in which all must co-operate if it is successfully to be given legal form,[5] but also implies a distinctive identity which can be perceived by others, for which no one needs either to be ashamed or to offer excuses. This in turn has to do with the self-esteem of the individual, which is not least dependent on the acceptance of others. Anyone who is humiliated daily cannot – to use Ernst Bloch's language – 'learn to walk upright', far less find a home.

Tendencies in both society and the church have been converging for some time over this programme for multicultural social life. At the same time it has to be pointed out that both in society and the church reservations have been expressed, for different reasons and out of different interests, about the project of multiculturalism, and attempts have been made to prevent it. It cannot be ruled out *a priori* that the mechanisms in play within a multicultural society in the perception of the alien and in behaviour towards others can also be found in the church, despite theological arguments and all the good intentions to make things different and better. However, the situation cannot be reduced to this. The programmatic concept with which a multicultural Christianity is sought for and discussed today is 'inculturation'. Inculturation is understood as the church's concern to introduce the gospel into a particular social and cultural context in such a way that people can believe in their own values in this sphere, in so far as they are compatible with the gospel.

II. Inculturation – into which culture?

It can be helpful to treat questions about the inculturation of Christianity against this background of multiculturalism, because it forces us to be realistic and to be careful about handling an explosive problem. Until an effort is made to explain more closely precisely what is to be inculturated where, we shall not get further than the current talk about the need for an inculturation of Christianity, which tends to have an inflationary effect. The situation is hardly changed if it is said that new evangelization has to emerge 'from a cultural reality'. Has there ever been an evangelization which has not emerged from a culture? Granted, the reference is now to indigenous cultures and their riches, in contrast to Western cultures. But who determines the 'true values' (or 'the spiritual and moral truths . . . and social life and culture', as *Nostra Aetate* 2 put it) of these cultures, and by what criteria can such a determination be made? Occasionally the distinction is put even more bluntly: evangelization should emerge not from a ruling culture but from an oppressed culture. However, that is no less problematical. First, the distinction between ruling and oppressed cultures is too simple, since each culture contains repressive and liberating elements (for example, are not women also oppressed in indigenous cultures and should the evangelization of culture take place from the perspective of these oppressed women – or if not, from whose perspective?). And secondly, quite apart from that, talk of dominating and dominated cultures seems to know the results before any analysis and argumentation.[6]

There are many sides to the problem of inculturation, so approaches to it and talk about it need to be differentiated. This differentiation is needed in closer definitions of what the gospel is and in a clarification of the hermeneutical question as to how far it is inevitably bound up with particular cultural traditions.[7] But more than that, the very definition and critical perception of culture raises difficulties. What belongs to a culture and who defines all that belongs to it? Who are its subjects? For example, T. S. Eliot defined culture as 'the whole way of life of a people, from birth to the grave, from morning to night and even in sleep'.[8] Coming from another perspective and using illuminating arguments derived from everyday happenings, D. Irarrázaval talks of a 'counter-culture of violence and death'.[9] One person's dream is another's nightmare!

If we are to avoid an ethnocentric understanding of culture on the one hand and a random cultural relativism on the other, then we must think of culture neither unequivocally or equivocally, but analogically. 'Analogy enables each participant to listen to, learn from, and eventually even partly appropriate alternative cultural visions of human value and possibility into her/his own horizon. The analogical mind learns to develop analogies which allow one to differentiate, to appropriate, and eventually to integrate a different vision of reality from one's own. As an entire community learns these analogical skills, ethnic pluralism – including its theological expressions – becomes not a threat but a promise: a promise of an enriched cultural self-understanding for all persons; a promise to develop a community-wide analogical vision embracing the diversity of several cultural heritages.'[10]

Neither churches nor theologians, wherever they may be, are immune from clichés in their perception of the other and the alien – to put it in more technical language, from stereotypes of aliens. The mechanism of ethnocentricity or sociocentricity which is at work everywhere can also affect them. This elevates 'the distinctive element, the world-view which is cherished in a particular social group, whether tribe, people or cultural circle . . . to a universal criterion: what is other and alien is repudiated as of lesser value, perhaps even as threatening, or is idealized as a paradise when one is discontented with one's own circumstances.'[11] Such stereotypes are at work when we speak of 'the Germans' or 'the Americans', 'Blacks' or 'natives', and they can be noticed not least in the discussions about the inculturation of Christianity which are being carried on at present. This is all the more understandable since the missionary methods with which Christianity spread in the wake of colonialism and imperialism, contrary to other slogans, were not concerned to recognize other cultures and religions – one need only recall the 1659 instruction of the Propaganda Congregation. On the contrary, convinced that they knew true humanity and were in full possession of the truth, Western churches and theologians were not afraid of annihilating other cultures by force and demonizing alien systems of religion. So in this connection it makes sense to speak of a hermeneutic of subjection as opposed to a hermeneutic of recognition. A mere glance at mission history produces a bad conscience which can hardly be remedied even by the numerous 'exceptions' of successful encounter and unconditional recognition of the other. The mechanism mentioned above can again play a role in remedying this situation, which the quincentenary of the discovery of the Americas has helped to illuminate, but in different circumstances.

If at one time an uncritical identification of Western Christianity with the gospel led to theological vandalism, today a 'transfiguration of cultures', bound up with an 'allergy' to Europe or the West, can perhaps lead to a theological romanticism which sees only the positive element in the cultures of others and hardly dares to make critical remarks any more, because they could hurt someone again. So it has rightly been pointed out that this is the same 'epistemological arrogance' which has to have the last word in judging other cultures, even if this word for the moment sounds positive. Whereas earlier what was alien and others was branded 'barbarian' and 'pagan' and condemned, today it is celebrated as being good and noble. If such an attitude is not prepared to differentiate, it is dangerous, not least politically (and it is dangerous for the church). Pleas for the rights of others in their otherness made in a multicultural euphoria without a closer definition of the content of this otherness, and hymns of praise sung to difference,[12] can easily turn into the opposite of what is intended. Unreason also has its deceit! Surely we must think hard when nationalists and contemptuous fundamentalists heedlessly use the same argument to claim their right to refuse to discuss multiculturalism and to trample to power over dead bodies? Their argument then is simply, 'If others have the right to be different, why don't we?'

No one will seriously be able to question the urgent need for inculturation. But how we deal with the problem calls not only for theological and hermeneutical sensitivity but also for something even more basic: respect for the others as 'subjects who have come of age' and substantive discussions. In particular we have to listen to the voices of those churches outside Europe which had to suffer the cultural alienation that the straight-line export of Western Christianity produced among them. We are warned by them, among other things, that we are infected with an 'inculturation fever as a desperate last-minute attempt to give the church an Asian façade'.[13] What is to be done if those involved do not themselves feel that the problem of inculturation is an urgent one, and there is less interest in traditional culture than in a 'Western way of life'? Can inculturation sustain a fragmenting cultural heritage and even raise up submerged cultural traditions to new life? Can the inculturation which is being called for meet the increasing impoverishment which it seeks to avoid? Empty words do not fill hungry bellies. Often we do not hear from those involved about their needs, but from Western missionaries, theologians and church representatives who talk to one another about inculturation and occasionally even know precisely what is to be inculturated and how. Church members are then expected to accept that what these people find good or bad in their culture is indeed good or bad. The old charge of missionary paternalism, of Western Christians exercising their domination over others in all things in life, is then justified. Here are the same methods as those with which the old colonial superiority is perpetuated, even if it appears in new garb.[14]

One thing is often striking in current talk about the inculturation of Christianity. Occasionally inculturation is spoken of with no indication of which culture is being inculturated into and with no identification of the subjects. Rather, the meaning of 'culture' is taken for granted. However, as I have already pointed out, this meaning is not clear. And the consequent vagueness also affects talk of inculturation. If we note what anthropologists have already been saying for some years, that there are now more than three hundred definitions of culture,[15] the need for restraint in this area is clear. Lack of concern can hardly be said to be a virtue, particularly if there are no obvious attempts at clarifying the subject and if the inculturation of the gospel is to be taken seriously. Into what culture is the gospel to be inculturated in a multicultural society? Into the culture of Catholic immigrants from southern Italy or Muslims from former Yugoslavia seeking asylum? Into the cultures of a racially mixed metropolis in South America or of an enclosed peasant village in a remote valley of a Swiss canton? What social strata are envisaged? Unemployed youth who meet to smoke grass in shady downtown areas, or people from industrial management who take time off to go to mass on Sunday? The questions are deliberately put as alternatives, but specific answers will be different in each case and will require pastoral options from the church. There is no doubt about it: the gospel is for them all, and the church has to do everything possible to see that this gospel comes to them as a liberating message and can find them in their identity. That already has consequences for the presentation of the gospel, as J. M. Tillard remarked: 'The gospel simply cannot be proclaimed in the same way in Jerusalem and in Athens, to a United Nations assembly . . . and to a gathering of poor peasants in Brazil. (Theological or doctrinal) pluralism is therefore connected not only with the culture in which faith is embedded, but also with its presentation . . .'[16]

Whenever inculturation is called for without a more precise focus on the culture envisaged and on those who hand it on or live within it, it unfortunately degenerates into a multicultural cleanser which is applied everywhere and from which some people evidently hope for a new outfit for the church without saying how this is to come about. It is not enough, as often happens, to appeal to a general definition of culture with recourse to statements of the magisterium (e.g. to *Gaudium et Spes* 53). Helpful though such a definition may seem at first, it is no help over the problem of inculturation as long as a concrete culture is not being analysed in its multiplicity of facets and conflicts. One can also practise inculturation bit by bit: a bit of music, a bit of popular wisdom, a few religious traditions . . . which are gradually received and transformed in a Christian way, because culture represents a totality. And already a further difficulty becomes evident. Even where cultures are analysed thoroughly (as in the case of indigenous cultures), they are mostly seen in too much isolation from other influential social mutations. When research is done into the internal logic of a system in order to be able to give a close description of culture,[17] external factors which define a culture tend to be blotted out, and as a result the culture itself is distorted.

So it is not irrelevant to raise the question whether results have to be expected from cultural analyses before inculturation can begin. But would not these come too late, because culture is a living reality and is constantly changing? And in the future would this not mean for Christian faith that it would have to become 'artificially natural and contrivedly spontaneous'?

III. Inculturation – a 'by-product'

If it is true to say that a Christian can be a Christian only in community, it is also important to stress that one does not have to live out one's faith everywhere, but at a particular time and in a concrete situation with its hopes and anxieties, problems and demands. Inculturation begins where people of different cultural traditions with their limited lives rely on the promise of the gospel, trust it and begin to live it out together for others by responding to the claim of the gospel and seeking to correspond to it in their everyday lives. But discipleship of Jesus of Nazareth cannot be had cheaply; it has its price for everyone, both those who call themselves Christians and those who want to become Christians. Those who commit themselves to the gospel cannot avoid leaving behind some things which they take for granted as part of their culture (cf. Matt. 10.39). Discipleship is impossible without a practice of deculturation if we are not to 'conform to the pattern of this world' (Rom. 12.2).[18] To discover what this means in detail calls for a 'discerning of the spirits'.

This everyday world has very different faces, and from the perspective of a community or its faith the challenges of faith are not the same everywhere. However, what should characterize Christian communities is their readiness to share the gospel with others beyond their limited circle and to show solidarity with all people. Where Christians begin to live in sympathy with their neighbours and to share their fate, that empathy can grow which is a necessary condition for understanding others and their cultures better, and possibly appreciating them. New human possibilites can be opened up, and one's own defects can be discovered. However, that does not happen *a priori*, but in the process of encounter with different people. The culture disclosed by concrete encounter with subjects who can be identified ultimately changes talk of inculturation, because it relates to particular people and their history, and thus leaves abstract matters of principle behind it. Yet this involvement must not be misunderstood; harmless though it may seem, numerous conflicts in society and indeed the church are programmed by it. Here we have a conflict not only of interpretations but also of interests, a conflict with which many Christians have to live.[19]

Inculturation cannot succeed without repentance in the sense of a radical renunciation of knowing better and asserting oneself, with the sole aim of reproducing one's own previous identity. This necessarily implies a capacity for self-renewal and requires an attitude of openness in which the values and defects of cultures alien to us are disclosed in free or unavoidable encounters with them from within, i.e. encounters with those who sustain them. The criteria used here must not be our own, if we are to do justice to the claims and self-understandings of others. The subjects of a culture themselves have the necessary competence to decide to what degree they find an authentic expression of their faith in the gospel communicated through concrete missionary testimony, where they experience alienation and where they can find their identity. Where this competence is denied or refused, the 'simple' and the 'babes' find their own way of expressing their faith. The religion of the people, popular religion, and the intensified movements of independent churches, bear manifold witness to this.

If it is not itself to compromise the concern for inculturation, a community of faith which wants to take multiculturalism in its own ranks seriously cannot leave out or suppress fundamental conflicts like the North-South conflict, racial conflict or the conflict between the sexes. The church has made its own contribution to these conflicts and they are also being fought out within it. The church is not only asked where it stands in these conflicts and what role it plays, but also how it deals with power. If one community does not want to elevate itself above the others, if communion is really to be achieved and not just asserted formally, then conflicts must be accepted and tolerated and their causes must be removed. Only then does an intercultural learning become possible which goes beyond a mere exchange of pleasantries. That requires of everyone no less than 'an eschatological respect for one another, a mutual recognition which cherishes solidarity even in the midst of conflicts'.[20]

Translated by John Bowden

Notes

1. O. Schumann, 'Die Fremden als Herausforderung. Der asoziale Geist des westlichen Denkens', in *'Fremde rause?' Fremdenangst und Ausländerfeindlichkeit: Gefahren für jede Gemeinschaft*, ed. R. Italiaander, Frankfurt am Main 1983, 48.
2. W. Huber, 'Viele Kulturen – eine Gesellschaft. Multikulturität in europäischer Perspektive', *Zeitschrift für evangelische Ethik* 36, 1992, 112–24: 112f.
3. F. X. Kaufmann, *Religion und Modernität. Sozialwissenschaftliche Perspektiven*, Tübingen 1989, 211. Cf. K. Gabriel, *Christentum zwischen Tradition und Postmoderne*, Freiburg, Basel and Vienna 1992; N. Mette, 'Gemeinde-werden im europäischen Kontext', in *Die Kirchen und Europa. Herausforderungen und Perspektiven*, Lucerne 1993, 125–39: 130.

4. B. Winkler, 'Kulturpolitik für eine multikulturelle Gesellschaft', in S. Ulbrich (ed.), *Multikultopia. Gedanken zur multikulturellen Gesellschaft*, Vilsbiburg 1991, 293–7: 294.

5. Huber, 'Viele Kulturen' (n. 2), 113f.: 'Respect for human dignity in the person of the alien, tolerance towards his or her forms of life, non-violence in resolving the conflict between different claims to truth, are decisive conditions both for pluralistic society generally and for multicultural society in particular. So it rests on a process of accepting the elementary rules of a community regulated by law which makes possible and safeguards mutual recognition. These rules cannot be framed in the name of multiculturalism: a consensus must be arrived over them from among the cultures. Thus the discussion about "core values" is an important topic of multicultural society . . . The fundamental experience for this formation of "core values" lies in the development of modern democracy, especially in the formulation of human rights.'

6. Cf. C. Rodrigues Brandão, 'El arca de Noe. Apuntes sobre significados y diferencias respecto a la idea de Cultura', in *Culturas y Evangelización. La unidad de la razón evangélica en la multiplicidad de sus voces*, ed. P. Suess, Abya-Yala 1992, 25–45: 43.

7. Cf. F. Wilfred, 'Inculturation as a Hermeneutical Question. Reflections in the Asian Context', *Vidyajyoti* 52, 1988, 422–36: 423: 'The efforts made at inculturation since Vatican II have been . . . largely of a pastoral nature. The theology animating these efforts has been mostly a theology of incarnation which is quite valid but, in my view, inadequate. The key question in inculturation is hermeneutical, and as long as we do not realize this, our discussions and debates on inculturation are bound to move within narrow limits: they may produce a lot of heat, but little light.'

8. T. S. Eliot, *Notes towards the Definition of Culture*, London 1948, 31.

9. D. Irarrázaval, 'Inculturación latinoamericana de la catequesis', *Medellín* 60, 1989, 542–76: 544; cf. id., 'Práctica y teologia en la inculturación', *Paginas* 122, 1993, 32–48: 33.

10. D. Tracy, 'Ethnic Pluralism and Systematic Theology', *Concilium* 101, 1977, 91–99: 96.

11. F. Gewecke, *Wie die neue Welt in die alte kam*, Stuttgart 1986, 61.

12. R. Darcy de Oliveira, *Elogio da diferença*, São Paulo 1991.

13. A. Pieris, *An Asian Theology of Liberation. Christianity in the Context of Poverty and the Religions*, Maryknoll 1987, 83.

14. Cf. V. Neckebrouck, 'Inculturation et identité', *Cultures et Développement* 16, 1984, 251–79.

15. Cf. A. L. Kroeber and C. Kluckhohn, *Culture. A Critical Review of Concepts and Definitions*, New York 1965, 291.

16. J. M. Tillard, 'Theological Pluralism and the Mystery of the Church', *Concilium* 171, 1984, 62–73: 71.

17. Cf. C. Geertz, *Dichte Beschreibung. Beiträge zum Verstehen kultureller Systeme*, Frankfurt 1987.

18. Cf. C. Burchard, 'Erfahrungen multikulturellen Zusammenlebens im Neuen Testament', in *Multikulturelles Zusammenleben. Theologische Erfahrungen*, ed. J. Miksch, Frankfurt 1983, 24–41; N. Brox, 'Fremdheit und Grenzüberschreitung im Frühchristentum', in *Das Fremde – Aneignung und Ausgrenzung. Eine interdisziplinäre Erörterung*, ed. G. Eifler and O. Saame, Vienna 1991, 15–33.

19. Cf. *La matanza de los pobres. Vida en medio de la muerte en el Salvador*, ed. M. Lopez Virgil and J. Sobrino, Madrid ²1993.

20. J. M. Bonino, 'Identität und Kommunikation', *Zeitschrift für Mission* I, 1975, 5–12: 11.

II · Test Cases

Coptic Christianity – The Process of Inculturation and Shaping the Coptic Identity

Maurice Assad

I. Introduction

At the heart of the Coptic community lies the Coptic church, as the cementing factor that continuously distinguished the Copts as a religious community. Its continuity has always been contiguous with the community, and symbolizes the characteristic of the Coptic identity.

The Coptic church has preserved its ancient tradition: its primitivity, mysticism, asceticism, piety and sacramental life. Religious rites and acts, in the Coptic church, have served as modes for communicating religious faith and life to the Copts. They have also been modes of inculturation that have shaped the Coptic identity. Coptic culture prevails in Coptic art, music, the architecture of Coptic church buildings and religious doctrine.

The Coptic monasteries supplied the Coptic church with an uninterrupted succession of patriarchs and bishops, who not only served the religious needs of the Copts but also assumed leadership of the Coptic community, in the face of persecution, intolerable taxes, or the discrimination to which the Copts were subjected from time to time throughout the history of the Coptic church.

However, the Copts – or the Christian Egyptians – have been living together with their Muslim neighbours since the seventh century. Together they have shared hopes and anxieties, and struggled against coercive rulers and their vehement and unbearable rulings.

From time to time, there were grievances between Muslims and Copts, but they never reached the level of enmity that would lead to social fraction between them.

II. The heart of the ancient world

In ancient history, Egypt represented the heart of the ancient world. The gates of Egypt opened, in the north, through the Mediterranean Sea, towards Europe. The Red Sea, along the eastern borders of Egypt, opens up towards the Indian Ocean. The vein of life, the River Nile, holds together central and northern Africa. Through these three waterways, the ancient civilizations in Africa, Asia and Europe were linked together and related to one another.

1. Unity of the land
The land of Egypt includes the Nile valley, the deserts to the east and to the west of the valley, and the Sinai Peninsula. The River Nile preserved and secured the continuity of the land. The Nile valley has been considered an enormous oasis in the midst of deserts to the east and the west.

The morphological unity of the land of Egypt, valley and deserts, and the functional unity that has been formed by the River Nile, preserved the continuity of Egyptian civilization. In the year 3400 BC, Egypt was born as one nation-state, which preserved its national unity and continuity throughout recorded history.

2. Name of the land
The name 'Egypt', now used in English and other European languages, was derived from the Greek *'Aigyptos'* and the Latin *'Aegyptus'*. Scholars suggest that the origin of this name was the expression of 'Ha-Ku-Ptah', which literally meant the 'the mansion of Ptah'. Ptah was the local god of Memphis, the ancient capital of Egypt for a long period of its ancient history. Hakuptah appeared in the Amarna Letters (1360 BC).

The ancient Egyptians called their homeland 'Kemyt' or 'Kimet', which means black: 'The Black Land', i.e. the fertile soil of the Nile valley. In the Coptic language, the name for Egypt is 'Kemi' or 'Kimi'.

Today, the Egyptians call their land 'Misr'. The word 'Misri' appeared in the Amarna letters. In the Hebrew text of the Bible, Egypt is called 'Misraim' or 'Musri' (see Genesis 10. 13; I Kings 10. 28–29).

The terms 'Copt' and 'Coptic' have been used since the seventh century. The Arabs called Egypt 'Dar-El-Kibt' (The House of the Copts). Some Arabic and Semitic sources indicate that the term 'Copt' was derived from the name 'Caphtorim' or 'Kuftaim', the son of Misraim, one of the grandchildren of Noah (Genesis 10. 1–14). The Christians of Egypt are now called 'the Copts', and their church 'the Coptic church'.[1]

3. The ancient Egyptians and their descendants

Some theories indicate that the early inhabitants of Egypt came from the South, from Africa, by land or through the Red Sea. Other theories believe that they came, from East Asia, through the Delta of the Nile. However, it has been confirmed that the ancient Egyptians were the autochthonous people of Egypt. They unceasingly continued to live on the land of Egypt from the pre-dynastic period to the present time. In spite of the subsequent invasions of Egypt by other nations and peoples throughout history, the descendants of the ancient Egyptians have been the same people during the successive stages of history, and until the present.

The inhabitants of Egypt today, the Egyptians, whether Muslims or Christians, are, in fact, of the same origin. Gamal Hamdan, a Muslim Egyptian anthropologist and geographer, who died recently in a sad accident, elaborated on this idea: 'It is not true that the Arab Islamic current uprooted the "Coptic" foundation to a pocket in the south . . . Recent anthropological studies proved the fallacy of the theory that differentiated between the "Copts" and the "Fellahin" (the Egyptian peasants) . . . In fact, the Copts and the fellahin are almost one and the same . . . This answers the common theory that says that the Copts represent the ancient Egyptians more than the Muslims. No doubt this is true, but only for some Muslims, and not for all of them. Arab blood was not necessarily mixed with the blood of all the Muslims. Hence, there are Muslims who are no less near to the ancient Egyptians than the Copts.'[2] One would add that such Muslims could be called 'Muslim Copts'.

4. The impact of ancient Egyptian religion and culture

Religion played a dominant role in the life of the ancient Egyptians. Through myth, mystery and symbol, they expressed the depth of their religious faith. They sought God through the natural forces that surrounded them. They believed that God existed beyond the material powers. The local deities, of the towns, personified the natural phenomena that affected their life. However, the sun and the Nile were the sources of life. The sun was identified with 'Horus', and was called 'The Sun-God Eye', or 'Horus-Eye'. The River Nile was identified with Osiris, who was considered the giver of life, the source of fertility. The Nile and the sun, Osiris and Horus, symbolized the struggle against corruption, destruction and evil. In ancient Egyptian mythology Set, the brother of Osiris, represented evil. Set killed Osiris, and Horus fought against the evil Set and restored his father Osiris to life. The tears of Isis, the mourning wife, assisted her son in restoring his father to life.[3]

The Osiris-Horus-Isis myth expressed the hopes and aspirations of the ancient Egyptians as they sought to develop a cosmic world view. The image of this affectionate and self-sacrificing triad has provided a model for the strong family ties among the Egyptians for more than six thousand years, during which monogamy has been the prevailing pattern among the Egyptian families.[4]

The ancient Egyptians believed in the unity of the deity. God for them was one, but he was known only through his attributes.

The concept of God as developed by the ancient Egyptians was related to their understanding of the human person as body and spirit. They believed in the immortality of the soul, and in the life hereafter, or life after death. They developed a psychology of life and death. Earthly or terrestial life was correlated, in their view, to celestial life or the life hereafter. They did not separate the material world and the spiritual world. They believed in the resurrection of the body and its faculties. The motionless body must be restored to the use of its members and senses. The 'self-power' of the deceased overpowers within him in the other world. Hence, he overcomes his own helplessness.[5]

They believed that the deceased person had to follow the process of the last judgment. He had to denounce forty-two sins, such as stealing, speaking lies, killing, committing adultery . . . etc. As the deceased appeared before the Great Court, he would assert his virtues: 'Behold, I come to you without sin, without evil, without wrong . . . I live on the righteousness of my heart . . . I have satisfied the God with that which he desires. I gave bread to the hungry, water to the thirsty, clothing to the naked.'[6] The deceased's heart was weighed in the balance against a feather, the symbol of truth.[7]

The ancient Egyptian psychology of life and death has affected moral values and behaviour until today. The Egyptians of the present day, without consciously realizing it, follow in the footsteps of their forefathers of ancient times.

Ancient Egyptian culture was interwoven with the religious faith and life of the ancient Egyptians. They were the first among the ancient peoples to create the principle of the alphabet, in which single symbols express individual sounds of the human voice. The creation of writing by the ancient Egyptians was an intellectual revolution to which the world is indebted to this day.[8]

Ancient Egyptian village life still prevails in many of the Egyptian villages today. The ancient Egyptian calendar, which was the basis of the Coptic calendar, is still used for identifying the agricultural seasons. The national feast of Sham El-Nessim, which is celebrated every year at Easter, is just one example of the continuity of Egyptian social life.

Ancient Egyptian culture echoed the faith and life of the ancient Egyptians, and left identifiable marks on the life of the Copts over many centuries.

The ancient Egyptians reproduced nature in art forms. They represented their gods in creative cosmic statues, in which they related the human form to animal, bird and natural forces (such as the sun or the moon). They represented their deceased in exact statues, in order to help the soul in identifying its own body. One could argue that Coptic churches carry some imprints of the architecture of ancient Egyptian temples.[9]

The pyramid was a unique creation of the ancient Egyptians; it stands as a witness to their advanced architectural methods. The place where the late President Sadat is buried, along with the unknown soldier, imitates the shape of the pyramid, in a simplified and reduced way.

However, the intellectual and literary advance of the ancient Egyptians lay in recording their history, in writing religious texts, in inventing stories, in stating moral and cosmic philosophy, etc. *The Book of the Dead*, *The Pyramid Texts* and other papyri taught Pythagoras and Plato the principles of mathematics and philosophy. The Egyptians also left their mark on Coptic literature.[10]

III. Shaping Coptic Christianity

In the Coptic Museum in Cairo, the visitor encounters a striking icon: the Virgin Mary riding on an ass, St Joseph carrying the child Jesus on his shoulder, with one leg to the front and the other to the back. Joseph supports the child with one hand and the other hand holds the rope tied to the donkey. It is not uncommon to see similar scenes in Egyptian villages today. As Egypt welcomed the refugee Jesus, it also welcomed St Mark, the writer of the Second Gospel, who is the founder of the Coptic Orthodox Church, in AD 68. He was martyred in the streets of Alexandria in AD 68.

The successors of St Mark carried the Christian message all over Egypt.[11] Some scholars attribute the rapid spread of Christianity in Egypt to the parallels between Christianity and the cult of the triad Osiris-Isis-Horus mentioned above. Christianity gave the Egyptians new hope for salvation from the aimless and dull life under Roman rule. Only future comfort and spiritual solace in the next world remained, and this Christianity promised.[12]

1. The intellectual challenge

When St Mark came to Alexandria, he found Greek philosophers, Jewish thinkers and the remnants of ancient Egyptian scholarship interwoven. According to Coptic tradition, St Mark founded the Catechetical School of Alexandria in order to combat their teachings. The teachers and students lived together, and shared worship, fasting, celibacy, and biblical and theological studies. The Coptic seminaries today attempt to follow the steps of the great teachers of the School of Alexandria, such as Pantaenus, Athenagoras and Clement.[13]

During the first four centuries, converts to Christianity were taught the principles of the Christian faith, using the *Didache*, or the *Teaching of the Apostles*, reading the scriptures and participating in 'the liturgy of the catechumens', before baptism.[14]

2. Coptic, Romans and Byzantines

During the Roman rule of Egypt (30 BC–AD 641), Christianity contributed to the revival of national identity among the Egyptians. The Copts found in their patriarchs the leadership they needed in their struggle against the Romans and the Byzantines. In his struggle against Arianism, St Athanasius (296–373) was also fighting against the Byzantine emperors. He was exiled five times from his see in Alexandria, the first time by Constantine himself.

At the Council of Chalcedon (451), the Egyptian church lost the leadership among the ancient churches. Egyptian patriarchs presided over the ecumenical councils of Nicaea (325), Constantinople (381) and Ephesus (431). At Chalcedon, Dioscorus, Patriarch and Pope of Alexandria, faced the power of the Pope of Rome, Leo I, and the tyranny of the empress Pulcheria and her husband Marcian. The Copts never accepted a Greek patriarch to replace their beloved Pope Dioscorus, who was deposed from his see and exiled by the Romans.

From Chalcedon until the Arab conquest of Egypt in 641, the Byzantines continued to impose Melkite Greek patriarchs upon the Copts, who were never accepted by the Egyptians. The Coptic church continued to select and ordain its patriarchs from among the monks of the Egyptian monasteries.

In order to enforce their domination over Egypt, the Byzantine emperors appointed the Greek patriarchs as rulers of the province of Egypt at the same time. During that period, Coptic clergy were executed; Coptic patriarchs had to escape from Alexandria and continue their ministry from their hiding places among the monks in the desert. Worshippers in the Coptic churches were frequently attacked during church services. Coptic church buildings and properties were given to the Greeks.[15]

3. The Copts under Arab and Turkish rule

At the time of the Arab conquest of Egypt (641), the Coptic population, the inhabitants of Egypt, was estimated to be twenty-four million. By the end of the ninth century, they were no longer the majority, and by the fourteenth century they were reduced to one-tenth of the total population of Egypt. They suffered persecution at times, and responded by rebelling against the oppressors, particularly during the time of Al-Maamun in 830.

During the first three centuries of Arab rule, the Copts enjoyed relative religious liberty. Some Copts received the highest honours and titles of the state. Coptic art and literature, liberated from Greek influence, found free expression.[16]

The age of the Crusades (1095–1291) was one of the greatest calamities that befell the Copts, along with other Christians of the East. The Muslims opposed the Copts as 'worshippers of the Cross', and the Crusaders looked upon the Copts as 'outcasts and schismatics, worse than heretics'.[17]

The rule of the Ottoman Turks of Egypt (1517–1840) was one of the darkest periods of Egyptian history, for Muslims and Copts alike. Poverty and plagues reduced sharply the number of the Copts, as well as the total population of Egypt. The political system of the Ottoman Empire treated the Copts, along with other minorities, as autonomous groups, who were called 'millets'. The Patriarch of the Coptic Church was held responsible for administering spiritual and religious, as well as judicial matters, such as marriage, divorce and inheritance.[18]

The Copts lived for centuries, during the Middle Ages and until the nineteenth century, as part and parcel of the Egyptian population. Although they had no say in political matters, they were indispensable in the life of the Egyptian society. As a religious community, they continued to preserve the spiritual, moral and cultural values which made up their Coptic identity.

The Arabization of the Copts had been a gradual and long process. The Coptic language, the last stage of the ancient Egyptian language,[19] continued as the language of communication among the Copts until the sixteenth century. The transition from Coptic to Arabic took a long period of time, in which Coptic and Arabic intermixed, and borrowing from one language to the other was not uncommon. From the tenth century AD, the Copts compounded their writing in Arabic. Today, the Coptic language is used in the Coptic church as a liturgical language. Coptic and Arabic are being used alongside each other in worship.[20]

4. Sharing in shaping Modern Egypt

A long and bitter struggle for survival may be expected to leave behind an exhausted community. But the Copts, through their determination for revival and renewal, have always found refuge in their deep faith and spiritual life. They have continuously discovered new meanings to enforce the relevance of their religious tradition. The rise of modern Egypt as a nation-state, and the development of modern ideas in social, cultural, educational, economic and political life, which were initiated through contacts with the West in the nineteenth and twentieth centuries, were the context for a radical reform in the Coptic church.

Coptic leaders fought, along with Muslim leaders, against the British occupation of Egypt that took place in 1882. Together, they formed the *wafd* party, which led the struggle against the British. National unity was symbolized by a crescent embracing a cross, and was expressed in the statement 'Religion is for God and the nation is for all'.

The Copts also participated in developing intellectual leadership, in the fields of medicine, science, engineering, accounting, history, philosophy, psychology, literature, education and law.[21]

The 1952 revolution, which was led by Gamal Abdel Nasser, brought about radical changes in political, economic and social life of Egypt. Through the practice of 'socialism', it attempted to separate between religion and politics. With the suppression of 'The Muslim Brotherhood,' religion and religious leaders were confined to religious and spiritual matters. At the occasion of laying the foundation stone of St Mark's Coptic Orthodox Cathedral, in which Nasser participated with Pope Kyrellos VI, the Coptic Patriarch, Nasser said: 'God never called for fanaticism, but called for love . . . We all know of quarrels that happen in villages and other places. A Muslim fanatic stands up and incites the people, or a Christian fanatic stands up and excites the people, and brothers begin fighting one another . . . We must exort the fanatics, Muslims or Christians, to follow the right path . . . The world was created and along with it fanatics and fanaticism. The world will end and fanatics will be in it until the end.'[22]

When Anvar El-Sadat succeeded Nasser as President of Egypt in 1971, he adopted an open policy in politics and in economics. At a meeting to which he invited both Muslim sheikhs and Coptic bishops, headed by Pope Shenouda III, in 1977, Sadat said: 'We lived together for thousands of years on this land and beneath this sky, in an atmosphere of tolerance, and our sons and grandsons shall follow suit until doomsday . . . Every so often a rash act might be committed by one faction or another, but we always unite to put an end to it and contain it.[23]

However, Sadat committed a grave mistake by imprisoning leaders of the opposition parties, some Muslim leaders and some bishops and priests. Sadat was assassinated by the same Islamic groups that he had earlier encouraged.

Since 1982, President Hosny Mubarak has attempted to strengthen the democratic institutions. But Egypt today faces grave socio-economic problems: the population explosion, unemployment, national debts, violence, extremism . . . to name only a few of the problems that all Egyptians, Christian and Muslims, have to encounter today.

IV. Powers of inculturation in Coptic Christianity

The Christian person, living in a non-Christian context in Egypt, recognizes himself as a Christian only through the Christian community. He gains his Christian identity first in the home, even before knowing the church. The sense of belonging to the Coptic community becomes a spiritual force that distinguishes Coptic Christians with certain moral and spiritual values that guide them in their life and action. In fact, the impact of home and church is intermingled, in the life of the growing Copts, with the impact of other societal and cultural forces.

Hence, the Christian identity of the Coptic person is being within the life of the Coptic Church. His identity as an Egyptian citizen is shaped through education, communication media, peer groups and neighbours, and, in general, through the cultural milieu and norms prevailing in Egyptian society. The Egyptians, Muslims and Christians, live together, next door to each other; the church faces the mosque, and the call for prayer from the mosque's minaret is tuned with the sound of the Coptic church bells. The Muslim goes to his mosque, and the Copt goes to his Coptic church. They live and work together. Their customs and habits are the same. The religious heritage of each of them has interacted with the religious heritage of the other.

1. Tradition of One God in Trinity

Tradition is the living memory of the church, upon which its life, doctrine and structure are grounded. It encompasses the past, the present and the future, and represents the unity and integrity of the Coptic church. Tradition includes the written word and oral teaching. The Bible, however, lies within tradition as the source of authority in faith and life. The Bible is the part of written tradition upon which the church builds its authority.

The Fathers of the Coptic church rejected any formula for its Orthodox faith other than the expression of St Cyril the Great, 'One nature of the Word of God Incarnate'.

The Coptic Christian, living in a non-Christian milieu, emphasizes the Oneness of God in Trinity. This understanding is based on the Nicaeo-Constantinopolitan Creed: Father-Son-Holy Spirit, the One God. Upon this understanding, the whole church is united in *koinonia* with the communion of saints.[24]

2. The process of inculturation in Coptic liturgy

The *koinonia* finds full expression in the Coptic liturgy, which is the collective act of worship in which the whole church participates in communion with God, with the congregation, with neighbours and with oneself. The fundamentals of the Coptic faith and life are expressed in the liturgies of the Coptic church. They are the vehicles of the faith that bring the whole church before God: priest, deacon and congregation.

The immersion of the baptized infant into the water marks the child's rebirth into the covenant. Baptism indicates that religious education is not theoretical knowledge about God, but rather growth into new life and the experience of personal existence with God. The chrismation, the second of the seven sacraments in the Coptic church, is an integral part of the process of becoming a Christian.

However, the eucharist is considered the sacrament of the sacraments. It is the sacrament of the partaking of the living body of Christ. The liturgy of the eucharist is a journey into the faith of the Coptic church, and the entrance into the joys of the kingdom of God.

The congregation encounter a sense of the whole as they engage themselves in the liturgical events, acts, meditations and prayers. They offer prayers and petitions of thanksgiving to God and pray for the church and the world, the living and the dead. Receiving the communion is the climax of the eucharist, by which the communicant participates in the glory of the Kingdom of God.

The rich symbolism of the Coptic liturgy unites mind, body and spirit in the act of worship. Hence seeing, smelling, tasting and sensing participate in the act of worship, along with meditating, praying and learning. In other words, the external practices and expressions transmit a spiritual effect on the inner self.[25]

The other four sacraments in the Coptic church are confession, unction of the sick, marriage and priesthood.

3. Monasticism and Coptic piety

Coptic monasticism has set a pattern of spiritual life that has influenced the shape of Christianity, not only in Egypt, but also in the North and the East. The Egyptian deserts were holy lands, in which asceticism was practised and taught.

The greatness of the desert fathers lies not in what they said or did, but in what they were able to become. They seek self-understanding through the discovery of their true self. They seek God in their inner self, by means of purity, self-control and piety. The inward spirituality is developed through a long process of practising asceticism, and by struggling against evil. St Antony said to his disciples that the path to virtue is within the human self. 'Virtue exists when the soul keeps in its natural state . . . when it remains as it was created.'

The Sayings of the Desert Fathers illustrate the simplicity and the depth of their faith and life. They were humble and silent men, and did not have much to say. They replied to questions in few words, and to the point. Rather than giving an abstract principle, they preferred to tell a concrete story. Their brevity is refreshing and rich in content. The ideal of their life is purity of the heart. The theme of the sayings is not simple moral issues; it is rather the practice of asceticism, which is a continuous labour of the monk.[26]

Coptic monasticism has set the pattern of Coptic piety, not only among monks, but among Copts in general, from generation to generation, and from century to century. Coptic families unceasingly visit the Coptic monasteries, where they are continuously welcomed by the monks in the guest-houses attached to the monasteries. These serve as retreat places for Coptic families and individuals, who seek spiritual renewal and continuing growth in the life of piety.

4. Nurturing the faith in the Coptic family

The stable structure of the ancient Egyptian family was baptized in Christianity.[27] The oneness of Coptic marriage has been sacramental:

what God has gathered together will not be separated by men. Marriage in the Coptic church is the fulfilment of the union between God and humanity. In other words, 'the great mystery' of Christ's union with his church is symbolized by the union between husband and wife. The love between the two is equated with the love of oneself: the two becoming one self and one flesh. Hence, the Coptic wife is not a tool for the pleasure of the man, but the helper of her husband. Her dignity is expressed in her chastity before marriage and in becoming the glory of her home. Clement of Alexandria said: 'The mother is the glory of her children, the wife is the glory of her husband, both are the glory of the wife, God is the glory of all together.'[28]

Two major characteristics have distinguished Coptic marriage throughout the history of the Coptic church: monogamy and the restriction of divorce to the case of adultery. Coptic marriage is not contractual but sacramental. It is an organic oneness.

The life of the Coptic home offers the child an atmosphere that is effective in his inculturation and shapes his identity as a Copt. Coptic parents offer their children good examples of Christian life in their own lives. The father is a model of what it means to be a Christian, which the child seeks to follow in his own life. The parents nurture their children in Christian faith and life, and nourish them in the love of God.

Factors of change in Egyptian society have affected Coptic family life. Secularization, urbanization, mobility and immigration have changed its structure and the functions. The population explosion and employment go hand in hand. Communication media, particularly the television and the video, have weakened the moral and spiritual authority of the family.[29] The age of the computer offers new dimensions to family life, yet to be investigated.

New efforts are being made to preserve the stability of the Coptic home. In 1973, the writer of this article initiated 'The Family Life Education Programme' in the Coptic church. Conferences and consultations were held to develop family counselling. Special programmes were initiated for engaged couples, newly married couples and for the whole family. This programme continues to tackle family problems, including family planning and population explosion.

5. Inculturation through learning processes

During the Middle Ages, schools were attached to Coptic churches all over Egypt, where young children were instructed in reading and writing, both Coptic and Arabic, accounting, basics of the Christian faith, prayers and liturgical songs.

In the middle of the nineteenth century, the Coptic patriarch Kyrellos IV opened modern schools in which European languages were taught equally to boys and girls. Soon after that, many Coptic primary and secondary schools were opened all over Egypt, by bishops of the dioceses and benevolent societies of lay men and women. Until the 1950s, Coptic primary schools represented fifty per cent of primary schools all over Egypt. Church-related schools – Orthodox, Catholic and Protestant – continue to offer a quality education to their pupils and students, Christian and Muslim alike.

In the 1950s, two effective inculturation developments took place: offering Christian religious instruction to Christian boys and girls who attend government and church-related schools, and the rise of Sunday schools in the Coptic churches all over Egypt.

The sermon that is offered after the reading of the gospel during the Coptic liturgy has also been an effective means of inculturation.

Since 1962, His Holiness Pope Shenouda III has been offering his weekly teaching to five or six thousand members of the Coptic church, men, women, youth of both sexes and even children. The meeting has been divided into two parts, each of which lasts for forty-five minutes, with an interval of hymns. In the first part, the patriarch responds to written questions, dealing with personal problems and life situations. In the second part, he examines a biblical text, analyses a biblical theme, studies a biblical personality, teaches on one of the books of the Bible, or meditates on a psalm. The Bible, for Pope Shenouda, is not to be considered as a book of history. It is rather a book of faith and life. History books deal with events. The Bible deals with the condition of the heart. However, through the study of biblical events, we study the conditions of the human soul and human feelings and actions. Hence we enter into the depth of the soul and study its inner struggle. The Pope considers that when we study the Bible, we examine the human condition: relationship with God, with oneself, and with others.

In his lectures, Pope Shenouda speaks in a very simple, but eloquent, language. His carefully chosen words are of a very high quality. His wit and sense of humour contribute to the attractiveness and the effectiveness of his words. He is able to relate difficult meanings to simple minds. He relates biblical texts to life situations and personal problems. As the Pope speaks, each individual feels that his words are addressed to him or her personally.[30]

Likewise the bishops in their dioceses and the priests in their churches hold weekly meetings.

Notes

1. K. A. Kitchen, 'Egypt', in J. D. Douglas (ed.), *The New Bible Dictionary*, London 1962, 337; G. W., 'Kibt', in *The Encyclopaedia of Islam*, 1972, Vol. II, 990; A. J. Butler, 'Copts', in *Encyclopaedia Britannica*, 11th ed., Vol VII, 13; Aziz S. Atiya, *A History of Eastern Christianity*, London 1968, 16.

2. Gamal Hamdan, *Shakhseiat Misr: Dirasat fi abkareiat El-Makan* (The Personality of Egypt: A Study on the Geniality of the Place), Cairo 1967, 35–6.

3. James H. Breasted, *The Development of Religion in Ancient Egypt*, Philadelphia 1986, 3–48.

4. For further details see: Adolf Erman, *Life in Ancient Egypt*, New York 1971, Chapter VIII, 'Family Life', 150–66; Maurice Assad, 'The Coptic Family and Social Change in Egypt', in Masamba Ma Mpolo and Cécile De Sweemer, *Families in Transition*, Geneva 1987, 31–3.

5. Breasted, *Development* (n. 3), 52–62.

6. Ibid., 303.

7. Ibid., 304–5.

8. Edward Mcnall Burns, *Western Civilizations: Their History and Their Culture*, New York 1963, pp. 53–4.

9. Ibid., 55–60.

10. Breasted, *Development* (n. 3), 77–88, 293–305.

11. William Worrell points out that 'by the year 200 Christianity had spread greatly among the native Egyptians, and the delta was full of converts'. *A Short Account of the Copts*, Ann Arbor; Michigan 1945, 6, 8–10.

12. Atiya, *Eastern Christianity* (n. 1), 18.

13. Aziz S. Atiya, 'Catechetical School of Alexandria', in *The Coptic Encyclopedia*, ed. Aziz S. Atiya, New York 1991, Vol. II, 469–73.

14. Murad Kamil, *Hadarat Misr Fi El-Asr El-Kibti* (Egypt's Civilization in the Coptic Age), Cairo 1967, 72.

15. Martiniano Roctanglia, *Histoire de l'Église Copte, Tome I: Les Origines du Christianisme en Egypte: Du Judéo-Christianisme au Christianisme Hellénistique (Ier et IIe siécle)*, Beirut 1966, 137–50.

16. Atiya, *History of Eastern Christianity* (n. 1), 84–93: H. A. R. Gibb and Harold Bowen, *Islamic Society and the West: A Study of the Impact of Western Civilization on Muslim Society and Culture in the Near East, Vol. I, Part II: Islamic Society in the Eighteenth Century*, London 1975, 259.

17. Atiya, *A History of Eastern Christianity* (n. 1), 92–3.

18. Gibb and Bowen, *Islamic Society and the West, Vol. I, Part II*, (n. 16), 259; A. H. Hourany, *Minorities in the Arab World*, London 1947, 20–1.

19. Ancient Egyptian writing, hieroglyphics, was composed of pictographic signs, denoting concrete objects. Gradually, the signs departed from the objects and became symbols representing abstract characters. Characters were combined to form words. The Egyptians formed new signs for their writing, which is called hieratic. Further simplifications of hieroglyphics and hieratic writing formed demotic (about 900 BC). Under the rule of Alexander and his successors, the Egyptians used Greek letters and added seven letters from demotic to write their Egyptian language, which became known as 'the Coptic language'. See J. Cerny, 'Language and Writing', in J. R. Harris,

The Legacy of Egypt, Oxford ²1971, 197–219; E. A. Wallis Budge, *Egyptian Language: Easy Lessons in Egyptian Hieroglyphics*, New York 1966. Burns, *Western Civilization* (n. 8), 53–5.

20. The Arabic language became the official language of Egypt in AD 706. Present-day colloquial Arabic, used by the Egyptians, is the outcome of the intermixing of Coptic and Arabic. See Cerny, 'Language and Writing' (n. 19), 197–211; Willson B. Bishai, 'The Transition from Coptic to Arabic', in *The Muslim World* LIII, April 1963, 146–50.

21. Manfred Halpern, *Nationalism and Revolution in Egypt: The Role of the Muslim Brotherhood*, Stanford, California 1964, 162; Atiya, *History of Eastern Christianity* (n. 1), 103–12.

22. Translated into English by the writer, who participated in organizing this occasion.

23. Translated by the writer.

24. Maurice Assad, 'Mission in the Coptic Church: Perspective, Doctrine and Practice', in *Mission Studies, Journal of the International Association for Mission Studies*, IV–1, 1987, 27–8; part of this paper was published under the same title in *International Review of Mission*, LXXX, no. 318, April 1991, 251–61.

25. Ibid., 24–26.

26. Maurice Assad, *Education in the Coptic Orthodox Church: Strategies for the Future*, New York: Doctoral Dissertation at Columbia University 1970, 26–37.

27. See section II. 4 above.

28. Maurice Assad, 'The Coptic Family and Social Change in Egypt', 35. See also Maurice Assad, 'Family Life, Coptic', in *Coptic Encyclopedia*, Vol. 4, 1086–89.

29. Ibid., 31–57.

30. Maurice Assad, 'North Africa and the Middle East From the Eighties to the Nineties', in *Voices from the Third World*, Colombo 1989.

The Process of Developing the Church in Zaire: The Reciprocal Opportunity for an Encounter

F. Kabasele Lumbala

A church develops in the course of an encounter between Christ and a people through contingencies of all kinds. For Zaire, these contingencies include the Mediterranean cultures of the missionaries, colonization, and the quest by the Christian West for new markets. Since the fifteenth century, the Congo Basin has had the seed of the Good News, and over the centuries that seed has grown and borne fruit. There are now almost 17 million Catholics; 51 bishops and 1,100 priests who are indigenous; around 3,500 Zairean religious, 100 of whom are engaged in mission abroad; more than 50,000 catechists and responsible lay people in the communities; numerous research and experimental centres for theology, pastoral work and inculturation. This is surely 'the strongest Christianity in Africa'.[1]

I shall not relate here the history and statistics of the formation of the different Christian churches in Zaire; they can be found elsewhere.[2] Rather, I shall touch on the subject as it relates to the topic of this issue of *Concilium*: the encounter of the gospel with African cultures.

The Catholic Church will be prominent in this analysis. That does not mean that I do not recognize the importance of the other Christian churches or the role that they have played in the process of its formation. Furthermore, the churches of other countries in Black Africa will be echoed in this article, since the realities of the life of these churches overlap because of the vagueness, the artificiality and the mobility of the frontiers which we have inherited from colonization.

Two features seem to me particularly important in the formation of the church of Zaire: it is a church marked by colonization and centred on inculturation. So these features will shape the two main sections of the following analysis.

I. A church marked by colonization

It is a fact that the church of Zaire was founded by the Western missionaries who had accompanied the colonizers and explorers. That has left profound and lasting traces on it: continual compromise and confrontation with the secular administration; the presentation of it as an opportunity for Africans, i.e. as a church which develops principally through beneficence; and finally the prestige and moral power of the structures of the church for the people.

Along with colonization, Christianity used its methods of destroying indigenous cultures, in that baneful equation of evangelization with civilization. Since the aims of colonization were fundamentally disastrous for black people, who were considered 'inferior',[3] missionaries there were compromised to the point of legitimating colonization.

Certainly the colonists marked out roads, put in place an economic basis, built schools and health centres, and fought against the slaving campaigns. But they did this with a view to their own prosperity and the efficiency of their enterprises; and they made much use of the missions for this social framework.

The missions themselves benefited from colonization in being able to spread the 'good news'. Furthermore, to lump Christianity and colonization together would be a hasty oversimplification, even if we have to admit that the missions could not have been able to prevent colonization from profiting from them in its exploitation of the 'natives'.

For the mission theology of the time, not to become a Catholic Christian was to doom oneself to hell. It was also necessary to wage relentless war on the traditional African religions. These had the values of love of neighbour, prayers sometimes addressed to God but more often to ancestors, sacrificial rites, meals of communion with the ancestors, rites of purification, reconciliation and conjuration of evil during bad weather or epidemics, divinatory practices, and so on. The goal of all these practices was human life and its growth: these are 'anthropocentric' religions. But if human beings are respected, it is because they belong to God; life itself is considered sacred because it comes from God; good will be rewarded and evil punished; the supreme evil is hate, seeking death for others. Hence the solidarity and constant appeal to love in hospitality and reconciliation, as preventing evil.

To live with these values is certainly to be near to God and intimate with God. So what need was there to adopt another religion? We Africans who live only by our traditional religions would have lacked Jesus Christ and the biblical revelation of the Father.

The Bible reveals to us the infinite love of a Father whose image and likeness we are, who is so near to us that we can be unfaithful to him and offend him, whereas in our traditions this God is beyond our reach. The Bible teaches us that the world and its history are guided towards the realization of a divine plan; this plan has reached its climax in the incarnation, an unprecedented event in which God became man, assuming the human condition until death. All that was unknown to our ancestors. Christ also comes to reveal to us that there is happiness after this life, and that our earthly life is destined to 'pass', giving way to communion and dwelling in the life of God, so that finally we become 'participants' in the deity (II Peter 1.4). Finally, the fact that there is no other name under heaven by which one can be saved than that of Jesus Christ, made Lord to the glory of the Father, constitutes the newness *par excellence* of Christianity for us and our ancestors.

The Christian churches are continuing to deepen this message in the communities to ensure the cultural rooting of the faith; however, for some time too they have also had a revived awareness of the need for political freedom and the establishment of democracy: numerous martyrs of these struggles can be found in the ranks of the churches. One need only recall the marches of Christians on Kinshasa, the nomination of bishops to preside over 'national conferences' almost all over Central Africa and West Africa.

It should also be mentioned that in Zaire the churches are the only viable administrative structures, and that economic relief is often channelled through them; it is they which encourage and support numerous development projects in collaboration with non-governmental organizations.

There has always been compromise and tension between the administrative power and the ecclesiastical power. In colonial times, the missionaries had the status of administrative agents, rising as far as judicial power. But they sometimes had to oppose the colonists, for example over the exploitation of agriculture, the running of schools, and so on. The present-day bishops and priests of Zaire have inherited these missionary prerogatives, and tend to hang on to them. Sometimes priests wear soutanes at the frontier to ease their passage; our bishops put on purple to travel into the interior . . . The tensions between Mobutu and the late Cardinal Malula simply manifested this heritage of colonization, even if the 1971 situation included some complex elements relating to authenticity and Christian names. Numerous courageous documents from the episcopate have interspersed these tensions, for example *The Dawn of Independence* (1959), *The Church in the Service of the Nation of Zaire* (1972), *A Call to Redress the Nation* (1978), *Our Faith in Human Beings, The Image of God* (1981), claiming basic human rights, *Democracy in Peril*, and *A Further Effort to Save the Nation* (1993).

Marked by colonization, the church is mainly financed by gifts and capital from the West. Certainly, here and there Christians are urged to look after their priests; but how can Christians who eat on average once a day provide three meals a day, fuel and a vehicle for their priest? Moreover the subsistence of the parishes and bishops, their ordinary functioning, depends essentially on Western subsidies, and these essentially come through the ancient metropolis.

If a Zairean clergyman travels abroad, he needs not only the signature of his bishop or that of the Administrative Secretariat of the Episcopal Conference, but also an endorsement from the Secretary of the Nunciature. The economic power of the international congregations is such that bishops and priests from Zaire have to queue and bow and scrape at the gates of the mission procurators.

Terrorized by these paternalist structures, many bishops and priests behave in the same way to their flocks or their colleagues to the point that a theologian has called them 'terrorists'.[4]

II. A church centred on inculturation

The *ad limina* visit of the Zairean bishops in 1988 confirmed the option of inculturation as being that of the church's current mission in Zaire. It happens through the various functions of the life of a church (liturgy, catechesis, theological research, administration), in rhythm with the life of the communities and scientific research and in ecclesiastical institutions, with a concern to enrich the whole of Christian experience.[5]

1. *New rites and a new theological stake*

Unprecedented rites in the Western Christian tradition have emerged in Black Africa and particularly in Zaire, like the blessing of parents and the pact of blood in religious consecration and marriage, initiation rites for passing on power in priestly ordination, rites of passage in the baptism and confirmation of adults, rites for the conjuration of evil in the sacrament of the sick and the sanctification of time, rites of reconciliation in the sacrament of penance and reconciliation, invocation and veneration of ancestors in the eucharistic celebration, particularly in the Zairean mass.[6] The official recognition of the Zairean rite by Rome in 1988 is an important stage for the African churches. But is there anything new in all these rites?

The Christian Easter is the passage of Jesus from this world to his Father, a passage which saves us and gives glory to the Father. The African celebrations of Easter convey the same message, but emphasize the initiatory dimension of the event. Baptism celebrated with white kaolin, banana leaves in a mime of death and resurrection, still signifies new life in Christ. But there is an accent that these African symbols and gestures put on the theology of baptism; it is that of life as 'passage and initiation', and as participation.

In using local food for the eucharistic meal one is still proclaiming the death and resurrection of Christ as a saving act; but by using these local elements one is putting a theological stress on the actuality of the incarnation of the Word.

When one knows the dynamic of the binomial factor of faith and rites, one can understand how all these new ritual practices are capable of transforming Christianity, if not completely, at least by enlarging its scope and its approach. Would that not be an opportunity for Christianity?

2. A new Christian iconography

In 1970, a song by a Zairean musician called 'I ask questions' asked why God was presented as a White, the angels were always White, the saints were always White and only the devil was Black. The song was broadcast all over the place at the height of the 1971 crisis beteween state and church. It showed that there was a problem in the presentation of the Christian mysteries, and drew attention to the cultic images that Mveng had been producing in Cameroon since 1964.

The decoration of our places of worship has resolutely adopted African motifs to represent the saints and the Christian mysteries. This obeys not only the need for a catechesis but also a theology of the incarnation. Since God was made 'man', the representations of God's mystery in the cult must speak to people of every race, of every country and of all times. It is better to represent God and God's mysteries in the features of all the races in order to indicate better that they are not identical or limited to any race.

These Black Christs and Virgins represent not only African art, but the whole life of the country, a whole conception of the world and life, a whole way of believing and being Christian, and thus enrich the whole Jewish-Christian tradition.

3. Living differently as a church: the base communities

The experience of the base communities with their lay heads began with the plenary assembly of 1961. This option inaugurated a different way of living as a church, i.e. as a family, in an African style. People often recall the words of Cardinal Malula when he made this form of organization official for Kinshasha, words which had an explosive effect on the parishes. 'In former days European missionaries Christianized Africa; today, Africans are going to Africanize Christianity.'[7] In fact the 'parish' was no longer enough for the task of the church; Christians were rediscovering themselves in the heart of the places where they lived outside parish worship, by living as a church during the week. The prayer which is offered is an extension and deepening of Sunday prayer. So here is a cell which is conceived to give parish life an influence on houses and districts, so that all the problems of life are faced in the rhythm of faith.

But at the same time these communities are announcing the era of new ministries: the priest is no longer the 'chief' there, but the spiritual inspiration of the cell. All the administration and pastoral work lies with responsible lay people who exercise these functions as a group. They are chosen for the community, and they are married, because according to Bantu culture one does not give any social responsibility to anyone who is unmarried. How could someone who has not given life and does not have the responsibility of 'father' or 'mother' be a sign of the transmission and safeguarding of life, like the ancestors? The ideas of 'spiritual fatherhood' or 'spiritual motherood' sound empty in a society in which human beings form an indissoluble whole of body and spirit.

4. Another way of doing theology

Without doubt the centres of theological research make a good impression in Zaire: the debates on African theology, on which T. Tshibangu and Canon Vanneste made their mark, began there in the 1960s. The present Catholic faculties in Kinshasa are beyond question contributing to this research by teaching and above all by organizing theological weeks. But the fact that their function is too dependent on the West as a result of the appointment of certain individuals means that these faculties are not the spearhead of the formation of our churches. The base communities are the spearhead.

The different titles given spontaneously to Jesus Christ in the different songs composed by the base communities have traced perspectives for an 'African christology'.[8] To begin with, African Christians simply took up titles which in their traditional prayers they had attributed to God and applied them to Jesus Christ, in accordance with the message of celebration. This is evident in the hymn to Christ which takes the place of the *Exsultet* on Easter Eve: images familiar to the life and culture of our communities are set in a framework which conveys the message of a Christ who is conqueror, hero, supreme head, our Easter sacrifice, liberator, healer . . .

These 'African' faces of Christ constitute primarily an effort to interiorize faith, to give roots to the message so that it is no longer foreign, and to make African Christians feel at home in the church.

Finally, all these features are symbols which themselves unveil and veil, in other words do not say everything about Christ, since Christ remains outside all models. And that is one of the opportunities that Africa constitutes for Christianity; in its efforts to name Jesus, it takes account of the immensity of the mystery of Christ, thus forcing the Christian world to transcend the Western monolith in expressing salvation in Jesus Christ.

5. Ecumenism

Christian Africa has not experienced 'wars of religion'; it also constitutes a privileged area for a dispassionate practice of ecumenism. Current experiences are moving in the direction of a communion of churches rather than a return to a 'single' church. Christ's prayer 'that they may all be one' is not understood as a desire to 'return to the Catholic confession', but as a call to each of the confessions in the truth of its witness of love. The different confessions, like the different peoples, finally manifest the riches of the mystery by stressing one or other of its aspects. Even if sin was at the beginning of the separation, on both sides, God has finally triumphed over sin by giving each of the confessions particular gifts from which the other confessions can profit. These have become as it were different families of a clan, the clan of Christ; they have meetings during which they pray together, remembering their 'ancestor' Jesus Christ, hear his word and comment on it, each in turn, sharing with the others its manifold and inexhaustible echoes. Several groups are born and function outside any particular denomination, belonging to no church.

6. Oral catechesis

Here we are looking at oral techniques, in particular those favouring the word and living contact, which appeal to memorizing, to the use of images and symbols. These benefit from the inexhaustible treasure of stories, and by paying attention to the cosmic rhythm make the catechetical periods coincide with the major seasons of the year.

Such a catechesis relativizes written knowledge, and that is useful in a Christianity which is too often based on the manuals, to the detriment of live experience and oral transmission.

The parish of Cikapa-Kele in Kasayi is the most spectacular example: the ancestral stories are classified within the communities and recited depending on the relevance of their message to that of the chosen gospel, before the biblical readings. These readings do not follow the official and universal lectionary; the texts are chosen by the communities themselves to meet the problems which they are experiencing. The children's catechesis follows the models of the initiatory retreats of the African traditions in which stories of the history of our peoples and our values are mixed with the history of our salvation.

7. New mysticism and budding charisms

In post-Vatican Catholicism, there is an emphasis on the mystical dimension of prayer as an intimate union with God and self-abandonment to the breath of the Spirit. This is particularly beneficial, since there could be a risk of forgetting that prayer is more the work of God in us than our own work.

This enrichment of Christian prayer has led to other developments in Zaire, in the encounter between traditional religion and certain veins of Christian religion, thus developing a mysticism of the saints; the living faithful are thought to be 'inhabited' by these saints, who are there to communicate a message or care for the sick. Traditional religion holds that the ancestors and the Beyond continue to be preoccupied with the earthly community and also intervene directly in the terrestrial, living momentaneously in an individual. On the other hand, the secular current of the Christian tradition of the saints attests that thanks to their proximity to and intimacy with the Omnipotent, they come to the aid of the living on earth. This aid is felt with all the more effect and warmth as Zairean names like that of Anuarite Nengapeta, beatified by John Paul II in 1985, are mentioned in the cult.

The Christian mysticism which is developing in Africa is not encountered only in these particular phenomena. It also manifests itself in the spectacular blossoming of religious congregations in Black Africa. These congregations have emerged particularly with the increase in the number of Black bishops: these vie with one another in zeal to let new charisms flourish in their dioceses. Whereas in the West religious congregations are merging in order to be able to survive, in Africa they are increasing in number with the birth of new congregations inspired by Africanness who echo the Christian message in a special degree on African soil. Moreover, older congregations are renewing their spirituality, seeking to understand how Africanness can help them to be better followers of St Francis, St Dominic, St John of the Cross and so on.

Conclusion

It seems to me that the churches of Africa are at present crossing a threshold: 'daughter churches', they are passing on to the stage of 'sister churches', and are now in turn enriching those who once saw them grow. Is not such an encounter a reciprocal opportunity?

Translated by John Bowden

Notes

1. *Missi*, February 1989, no. 2.
2. P. de Meester, *L'Église d'Afrique, hier at aujourd'hui*, Kinshasa 1980; *Aspects du catholicisme au Zaïre*, CRA Vol. 14, nos. 27–8, 1981; the Bologna colloquium, *Église et histoire de l'église en Afrique*, Paris 1988.
3. Guy de Bosschere, *Autopsie de la colonisation*, Paris 1967.
4. B. Bobo, *Le diaire d'un théologien africain*, Kinshasa 1987.
5. Pansinya Monsengwo, *Inculturation à l'exemple du Zaire*, Kinshasa 1979.
6. See the synthesis in my article in *Église et histoire de l'église en Africa* (n. 2).
7. Cardinal Malula, *L'Église à l'heure de l'Africanité*, Kinshasa 1973.
8. Cf. the fine synthesis by G. Iwele, 'Mystique et christologie en Afrique', in *La mystique africaine*, Kinshasa 1993.

Christianity in Pakistan

Mariam Francis

In Northwest India, now called Pakistan, modern Christianity appeared with the Afghan war of 1840. There were many Irish in the English army, and priests were asked to assist in their spiritual and other needs. Till 1875 only Eurasian and some Indians of better educational class were looked after by missionary sisters, but the mass movement of conversion changed the focus of these missionaries toward the newly-born church emerging from humble origins. In the vast land of Hindus and Muslims many *Harijans, Mussalli*[1] and a few others were converting to Christianity. Today, out of 130 million Pakistanis officially two per cent are Christians, though many hold that the government census is not correct, and there are far more Christians than there are believed to be.

I. Problems and Experiences

Minorities in all countries have to put up with a certain amount of hardship. In Pakistan they have to struggle against two types of prejudices: religion and caste. Pakistan has an ideological birth and framework. It is difficult for the Muslim Pakistani to see how anyone outside the Muslim faith and its associated culture can be anything but a second-class citizen. Numerically, politically and culturally Christians are being marginalized.

Nationalization

The first blow to the Christian community came in 1973 when Zia Bhutto nationalized the Urdu medium private schools where the majority of poor Christians were educated by the church. When the government took the administration into its hands, catechism first started to be neglected and then vanished. The Muslim staff stepped in and Christian students were badly affected; they were neglected, ignored and sometimes taunted by sarcasm and outright discrimination. They were damaged not only intellectually but also psychologically. Islamiyat as a subject became obligatory for every student. Before this, convents and other church schools played a major role in bringing Muslims and Christians socially and culturally close to each other. These English schools have a considerably better standard of education. As a result of this close interaction, respect for each other's community was created. There used to be moral science classes where human values were implanted in the students, and people who have gone through these schools do recognize the values which were instilled in them. Though Christian schools (English medium) continue to be owned and governed by the church, there is increasing interference from government quarters. The curricula and the style of teaching have been forced to adapt to government measures. Where there was once peace, today there is a clear religious rift.

Separate electorate

On many occasions, public officials refer to the minorities as the 'sacred trust' of the country. This implies alienation rather than a feeling of being treated on a par with the rest of the people of Pakistan.

The status of minorities was legally reduced during President Zia-ul-Haq's martial-law tenure, when the first step toward separate electorates was introduced in 1985. Under this system Christians can vote only for Christian candidates. They are generally not interested in which party rules the country or what type of programme a party in power offers. Under the present arrangements there are 217 seats in the National Assembly, ten of which are reserved for minorities: each minority group elects its own representatives in a separate electorate for the national and provincial assemblies. Four seats are for Christians, four for Hindus, and one each for Ahmadis and the rest of the minority religions. In the provincial assemblies of the four provinces of Pakistan there are 23 seats out of 483, total strength.

In the joint electorate system, minorities still had some clout as representatives. The introduction of separate electorates meant that minorities were no longer assured the support and protection of powerful Muslims. Unfortunately some bishops and Christians accepted and praised the idea of a separate electorate. The reason behind this acceptance was not so much to help their fellow country-folk as to settle for the crumbs of prestige, honour and power that fall from the table of the bureaucrats.

The Shariat Act[2]

To secure the approval of religious fundamentalists, the most inhuman laws were imposed in 1982 with the Hudood Ordinance. This catch-all ruling allows the government, present and future, to do pretty much as it pleases, because the bill is so broad in its scope and so general in its terminology that almost anything can be done in the name of religion.

Some of the Shariat Act facets are these:

1. *The Law of Evidence*. The testimony of two women is equal to that of one man, which is based on the interpretation that a woman is half a man. The testimony of a non-Muslim is not accepted. This kind of discrimination has brought women and minorities to some bizarre situations.[3]

2. *Qisas and Diyat Ordinances*. Compensation is provided for, in the form of blood money, half for a Muslim female and a Christian male, but one quarter for a Christian female. These absurd laws have harassed people for years.

3. *Blasphemy Laws*: From 1980 to 1988 five amendments were made in the penal code stipulating punishment for blasphemy or for insulting the sentiments of Muslims. The important one for Christians is section 295C, added in 1986, imposing the death penalty or life imprisonment for the use of derogatory remarks against the Holy Prophet Muhammad.

Interestingly, before these laws were actually promulgated, the number of incidents of blasphemy against the Prophet were negligible. The sub-continent has traditionally been a harmonious land for many religions. With the penal code amendment 295C, such allegations have arisen with alarming frequency. The worst fears of minorities were confirmed when this law began to be regularly used to settle old scores, political disputes or as a ploy to undermine a rival in matters such as employment. As of this date, dozens of people have been accused and arrested. Two have given their life, butchered and killed by fanatics. One is in the death cell and others are in prisons awaiting judgment.

The Shariat Act harms Christians, as no Christian lawyer can appear in the Shariat court; only a Muslim judge can conduct a hearing of blasphemy cases. Even to go through the process means months, or years, spent in attending court hearings, paying lawyers' fees, and suffering untold mental agony which may leave permanent psychological scars. There is also the damage to the accused's means of livelihood – as long as the process continues, his business is suspended and he cannot earn enough to feed his family. And finally, it ensures that someone who has once been through the experience will never have the will to resist other encroachments on his rights.

The saddest thing about the Shariat Act is that it was passed quietly and in a hurry, with one third of assembly members, while Prime Minister Benazir Bhutto was away from the country on 15 May 1991. People are not happy with it, and the Shariat Act is condemned even by the Jamaat Islami,[4] who consider it a government bill, and not as far-reaching as they would want. The Shias[5] reject it because it conflicts with their own code of law. Almost all women's movements are deadly against it as their human rights are jeopardized.[6]

The national identity card

In 1992 there was a move to include a special religion column in the national identity card. The government explained that this was meant especially to identify Ahmadis[7] (a sect considered heretical by the orthodox), as their names are similar to Muslims. Though the column was intended to mark the Ahmadis, it in fact affects the Christians as well.

However, there was strong public reaction against the move. The minorities, but especially the Christian community, did their best to have the government reverse this decision. The laity were the first to take firm steps: they went on hunger strikes and work strikes. Processions with banners of non-acceptance came out everywhere. The opposition and the Pakistan Human Rights Commission joined the minorities and the decision was quietly rescinded. The strength, unity and perseverance of Christians was a sign of certain political maturity, and of hope for the future church in Pakistan.[8]

Inferiority

Inferiority is another painful problem for Christians. Most Christians are segregated from the rest of society both socially and religiously. In a society where Hinduism, with its caste system, had a great influence, manual labour in general and sanitary work in particular are looked down upon. Christians, by the mere fact of being involved in sweeping jobs in towns, or as kiln workers, or the bonded labourers of landlords, have come to the point of lacking all self-respect. The illiteracy, ignorance and religious fanaticism of many Muslims are also factors adding to this inferiority complex. The Christians' fear, their sense of alienation and inferiority, is verified many times over because in caste prejudice Muslims and even 'well-to-do' educated Christians are very particular about not eating and drinking from vessels touched by the lower castes. Such a degrading attitude reinforces an already poor self-image.

Christians take comfort from I Peter 2. 9–10 ('You may declare the wonderful deeds of him who called you out of darkness into his marvellous light. Once you were no people but now you are God's people'), but how many qualified youths, with degrees and diplomas in hand, are refused a job because they are Joseph, Thomas or Peter . . . ? At this point, questions arise from the International Declaration of Human Rights, to which Pakistan is also a signatory. The Human Rights Charter declares that all citizens are equal before the state and all will have equal chances for employment. (23, no. 1). The same words are repeated by national leaders (even Christians!) when in the name of a sacred trust minorities' rights are said to be safeguarded. The reality is quite different.

Coping

How then do Christians cope? They are often sustained by the example and words of Jesus: 'If the world hates you, remember that it hated me before you . . . If they persecuted me, they will persecute you too' (John 15. 18–20). The type of discipleship presented in the Gospel of Mark is the one that appeals most to Christians in Pakistan. Jesus seems to be in a hurry, putting stress on freeing people from all that holds them captive. It is as if he wants to finish his mission before his death, which is at hand. All along the way he teaches what is meant by discipleship: 'If anyone wants to be a follower of mine, let him renounce himself and take up his cross and follow me' (9. 34).

Perhaps this is why there is a great devotion to the Way of the Cross. For Sunday Mass the crowd is sometimes small, but for the Stations, in spite of heat and long distances, churches are packed. People's devotion is indescribable. In the suffering Jesus, Christians have a model for their own life. They see how he had already lived the life they are living now. They take strength from their Master to discover, in what they have to undergo everyday, the very path of discipleship.

The Pakistani Christian derives great strength and meaning from the Psalms. People love to recite or sing them during times of sickness, before going to bed, during parties and weddings. A few years back a study was done by the Theology and Spirituality Commission of the Major Superiors Conference on the Punjabi Psalms.[9] The study discovered that Psalm 23 (The Lord is my Shepherd), Psalm 121 (I lift up my eyes to the hills), Psalm 40 (I waited patiently for the Lord) and Psalm 50 (Have mercy on me, O God) were the most popular ones. The search went on to find reasons for this and the study concluded that Christians, in all the troubles they face, take refuge in a mighty and loving God who takes their side and cares for them.

The Frontier Post, a national newspaper, recently published a letter about religious bigotry, written by Mohd Ahmed Khokhar (20 June 1993). In this letter he relates how he happened to be in the market where an old cobbler attired in rags was pestered by a so-called Muslim priest who urged the old man to give up Christianity and become a Muslim. The writer intervened, telling the Muslim to leave the old man in peace. A hot argument followed, and a score of people gathered. Listening to the story, they too took the old man's side and asked the preacher to beg for forgiveness for bothering the old man, which he did reluctantly. The writer concludes saying: 'I cannot help saluting the old man, who readily forgave him and embraced him in a fatherly manner.'

Today, being a disciple in Pakistan demands this kind of living Christianity, enduring and forgiving.

Caste discrimination

Besides religious discrimination, the Christian minority suffers from caste discrimination. Christians in Pakistan remember that Jesus 'emptied himself to assume the condition of a slave' (Phil. 2.7), and that wherever the apostles went to preach, the poor and the lowly were the first to believe in the one who 'became a slave'. Instead of Christians becoming depressed and sad, they as outcastes should 'boast of their weakness' (II Cor. 11.30).

Yet bold would be the preacher who reminds his/her congregation of their origins. I don't think I ever heard these words of Paul to the Corinthians – so true of us in Pakistan (almost all of whom come from the low 'non-scheduled' castes) – proclaimed publicly, and owned by the community: 'Take yourself for instance, brothers and sisters, at the time when you were called: how many of you were wise in the ordinary sense of the word, how many were influential people, or come from noble families? No, it was to shame the wise that God chose what is foolish by human reckoning, and to shame what is strong that he chose what is weak by human reckoning. Those whom the world thinks common and contemptible are the ones that God has chosen' (I Cor. 1. 26–28).

It is truly difficult to be a disciple and follower of Christ, the slave. There is always more than enough trouble inside and outside the church community.

II. What have Christians added to the culture?

Many times, it often happens that in a great multitude one can point out at once the person who is a Christian. There is no physical sign that lets one know this, but there is a kind of attitude or way of comporting oneself that distinguishes him/her from others.

This recognition occurs where there are teachers working in government schools, nurses everywhere, people in banks or other jobs. Private Christian schools often have a rush for admission because of the way teachers deal with the children. Their commitment, sense of responsibility, dedication and honesty attract attention. There are thousands of humble, nameless people like this, but the community can also boast of those who are pre-eminent and famous and who have been honoured by the government for their services. We have Dr Ruth Pfau, whose life has been dedicated to lepers, or Sr Gertrude Lemmens, who has become the Mama of hundreds of handicapped and abandoned children. Both of them work closely with Muslim (and Parsi) organizations. Because of their examples, many other institutes on a philanthropic base have been started for needy people.

It is ironic that, though Christians are derided for being low-caste, their services to families as cleaners, washers, gardeners or drivers are sought-for precisely because of the gospel values mentioned above. In a corrupted structure where poverty is taking hold of the poor through concealed taxes and created needs, for Christians to believe and ask for 'daily bread' is not an easy task. Especially when the world in which they are living offers illegal ways to attain an affluent life.

It is true that no religion teaches one to do evil or to harm another, but Christians received a new commandment: to love one another as Jesus loved. We have believed in this love which forces us to believe in Jesus as our king and conqueror of our hearts. Now when everything is business, when money buys love, admirers, friends, and accessibility to the powerful, when one goes in the dark lanes to meet with common people, one's eyes are opened to see that 'there are 7,000 who have not bent their knee to Baal' (I Kings 19.18).

Relationship between the sexes in Christian worship, among youth, in many and varied programmes and courses, is a counter-cultural element in Pakistan, where separation and division into sexes is part of Islamic laws. The healthy atmosphere of male and female Christians does bring change in the society. Like leaven in the flour, wonders do take place. Here dialogue has played its role too. The two communities of Christians and Muslims, living shoulder to shoulder, have the same socio-economic problems. These are the areas of social justice, moral values, peace, development and freedom in which Christian and Muslims and both sexes make common effort for a better world.

In our cultural circumstances, to bear witness to Christ is to bring the word of comfort to heal society, and to speak that prophetic word which challenges the structure. It is to restore human dignity and to proclaim a shared life. In our culture of nobles and lowly, rich and poor with thousands of traditional bondages, our witness leads people in the exodus from non-person to person, from subhuman to dignified human beings.

In dialogue and witness we remember that social and economic progress gives freedom to share with others a faith which can be at home only where there is justice. The justice and peace commissions of the bishops and of the major superiors on a national and regional level are perhaps most active in entering the life of society to deal with the problems in an analytic and practical way.

III. How have faith attitudes changed?

We have inside us the roots of the beliefs of four thousand years, whether we believe it or not. This ignorance is evident in the superstition, xenophobia and mass paranoia so prevalent. The gospel has not been able to uproot evil traditions (witchcraft), from which we not only suffer but harm others too. Most of the time the Christian community thinks only of itself, angry if church aid is spent on poor Muslims, even though we believe firmly in the commandment of love. As a minority we resist assimilating the culture when this is perceived as 'Muslim'. Because of ill-treatment from some Muslims we take all Muslims as enemies, as dishonest and corrupt. In order to put behind us our humble origins we have adopted an exodus mentality, thinking ourselves, like Jews, to be the chosen ones and the rest fit for the fire of hell.

Yet we are being transformed by the culture and by Muslim influences in some way. We try to imitate their ways, putting loudspeakers on our churches, as they have loudspeakers on their mosques, without thinking of the social, physical and psychological results. Their current fundamentalism is influencing us strongly, in our way of looking at scripture, revelation, the fast and other religious observances, giving more importance to what is formalistic rather than the message which derives from them. About scripture we have adopted the same understanding as Islam: 'the Bible and the Qur'an have come down from heaven and are revealed so miraculously that not one iota can be changed even in their interpretation'.

Challenge

The challenge to the minority in Pakistan is to be prophetic, here, in our own situation, in our own church, in this overwhelmingly Muslim country. To be a community of brothers and sisters formed by a different way of thinking that is abnormal, disturbing and challenging to our society, to our culture, to our church. The challenge is to believe that minority is the gift we give to Pakistan and to the world church. If it is true that the world church of the future will be – if it is not already – a minority church, then the way we live out this minority could be very helpful. This is our gift: not anything that we do, but who we are and how we live out our minority.[10]

Notes

1. *Harijans* is the name Mahatma Gandhi gave to the untouchable caste; it means 'Children of God'. *Mussali* are low-caste Hindus who accepted Islam.

2. The Shariat Act is a law by virtue of which all the existing laws, economics, education and mass communication institutes are Islamicized. Cf. also Christine and Charles Amjad-Ali, 'The Shariat Act and the Democratic Process', *Studies in Interreligious Dialogue* 3, 1993/1, 28–47.

3. In Sahiwal, for example, a blind girl was raped by a rich man. The man was released on bail while the girl was condemned to be stoned. Women activists came out on the road, publicized the case, and stopped this sentence being carried out.

4. The Jamaat Islami is an ultra-orthodox, well-organized and politically active group founded by Maulana Mahdoodi.

5. Shia describes that branch of Islam which takes its origin from 'the party of Ali', the son-in-law of the Prophet.

6. Some of the women's movements are WAF (Women Action Forum), WAR (War Against Rape), ASR (Applied Socio-economic Research), and *Shirkatgar* (Women's Documentation).

7. The Ahmadis are a nineteenth-century sect founded by Mirza Ghulam Ahmed, and considered heretical by orthodox Muslims for their belief that Mirza is the last Prophet.

8. Cf. Bonnie Mendes, 'Looking Back at the ID Card Issue', FOCUS Supplement 1993/1, 13–17, for a detailed description of these events.

9. Cf. Jan Hoeberichts and Patras Yusaf, 'The Psalms and the Punjabi God Experience', FOCUS 1982/2, 75–86.

10. Chrys McVey OP, 'Being Dominican in Pakistan', *Newsletter*, Dominican Family in Pakistan, May 1993/1, 11–12.

Christianity and Inculturation in Latin America

Fernando Castillo

Theological and pastoral concern with the relationship between evangelization and culture is relatively recent in Latin America. This is so despite – as we shall see – the fact that the problem has been present since the beginning of the evangelization of the continent; it has indeed been one of the main challenges facing evangelization.

I. Evangelization and culture as seen by the Latin American bishops

The growing interest in the subject is evident from the increasing amount of space devoted to it in official documents from the bishops, especially the 'final documents' of the General Conferences of Medellín (1968), Puebla (1979) and Santo Domingo (1992). It is, however, notable that while these documents reflect a more or less generalized state of pastoral insights and concerns, they also show hesitations and difficulties in tackling the subject: reflecting on evangelization of culture or 'inculturation' in Latin America leads inexorably to a critical confrontation with the history of the church itself in its five hundred years of existence on the continent. And – as with all institutions – critical self-evaluation proves particularly difficult at official levels.

(a) At Medellín, the main concern was different: the situation of injustice, crisis and social conflict affecting the continent. Little attention was paid to culture. Nevertheless, anxieties on the subject of the relationship between evangelization and culture did make themselves heard (in the statement by Mgr S. Ruiz and the document on Social

Pastoral Planning). The subject was introduced from various angles: despite five centuries of Christianity, the actual religious situation showed evangelization to be incomplete, with the church only weakly embedded in the society of the continent; at present, changes are taking place at an increasing rate, and emerging as cultural and religious transformations. This shows the need for pastoral planning to be 'adapted to the cultural plurality and diversity of the Latin American people' (*Social Pastoral Planning*, 1). Somewhat surprisingly, Medellín seemed to see the main problem being posed by popular religiosity, which it recognized as 'the fruit of an evangelization carried on from the time of the Conquest' (*Social Pastoral Planning*, 2); this it saw as a form of religious expression that, though with positive values, was deficient as an expression of Christianity and, furthermore, was facing its own crisis with the spread of a more technological mentality.

Despite its limitations in tackling the subject, Medellín has to be credited with having taken a significant first step by realizing that the new cultural situation of Latin America poses a challenge to evangelization and by stating, too, that 'faith, and consequently the church, are sown and grow in the culturally diversified religious expressions of peoples' (*Social Pastoral Planning, 5*).

(b) At Puebla, the bishops devoted a whole section of the final document to 'The Evangelization of Culture' (nos. 385–443). The document itself left no doubt that the chief impulse for this came from Paul VI's *Evangelii Nuntiandi*. This document and Vatican II's Constitution on the Church in the Modern World, *Gaudium et Spes*, were the sources that inspired Puebla's concept of the evangelization of culture. By making evangelization its main theme, Puebla planted ideas that were to surface in theological-pastoral discussions in the years up to the Santo Domingo Conference, and reappeared in its conclusions. So Puebla had already said that Latin American culture was the product of 'the encounter' and 'intermingling' 'of the Spanish and Portuguese peoples with the pre-Columbian and African cultures' (409), and that 'from the sixteenth to the eighteenth centuries were laid the bases of Latin American culture and its solid Catholic substrate' (412). But the document warns that this cultural situation is changing rapidly and that Latin America is experiencing the advance or advent of urban-industrial culture, expressed in 'scientific categories' (414) and with pretensions to universal hegemony. In this culture, 'the city becomes the moving force behind the new world civilization' (429); this poses a great challenge to the church in Latin America, which has traditionally existed and evangelized mainly in an agrarian culture. Particularly disturbing for the church in this development is the advent of 'secularism', historically linked to the progress of urban-industrial culture, which puts forward an areligious view of human beings and the world. At Puebla, the bishops said that the church saw secularism as 'a threat to the faith and the very culture of our Latin American peoples' (436); the great challenge facing evangelization was to ensure that the inevitable passage to urban-industrial culture did not take place under the aegis of secularism.

(c) In the Santo Domingo document, the subject of the evangelization of culture takes up even more space: a complete chapter of the 'Conclusions', entitled 'Christian Culture' (a title rather likely to produce misunderstandings, but which the conference took from the Pope's opening address). For the first time, the term 'inculturation' of the gospel is used (230). The evangelization of culture leads to a process of inculturating the gospel. In other words, inculturation is the church's response to the challenge to evangelize culture. At the same time, however, the document stresses a tendency already observable in Puebla, which implies a narrowing of vision on evangelization and inculturation: everything is reduced to the sphere of the 'values' in a culture; inculturation then becomes recognizing the evangelical values retained by present-day culture, recognizing new values that accord with the gospel and inculcating gospel values absent from that culture. From this viewpoint, inculturation is reduced to an (undoubtedly ambitious) undertaking to moralize culture in accordance with Christian morality (or, rather, with a particular Christian morality). And, from precisely this narrow viewpoint, the document goes on to elaborate what appear to be criteria for inculturation: 'Cultural values: Christ the measure of moral conduct' (231); the 'pastoral challenges' (232–236), which amount to a listing of the moral problems affecting the continent, and the 'pastoral guidelines' (237–242), which focus on the formation of a moral conscience.

Faced with this approach, one might ask whether the reduction of both gospel and culture to a collection of 'cultural values' does not immediately place the problem of inculturation on terrain where the church is going to have some difficulty in accepting and taking on the diversity of cultures and their 'otherness' in comparison to what seems pre-ordained to be 'what is Christian'.

Santo Domingo did broaden and deepen the magisterium's thinking on indigenous, Afro-American and *mestizo* cultures in Latin America, suggesting ways to inculturate the gospel in them, stating that evangelization should contribute to strengthening these cultural identities and committing the will of the church to supporting the human advancement of the peoples who bear these cultures. But at the same time, Santo Domingo recognized that, beyond its culture diversity, the continent is 'marked by Western culture', which the document also designates 'modern culture'. It was less timid than Puebla in confronting this modern culture and, especially, the 'secularism' it can bring.

This short survey of the documents issued by the bishops' conferences shows not only how concern for inculturating the gospel has become more explicit, but also the variety of aspects involved in dealing with this question, as well as the hesitations and limitations of the bishops' proposals. These documents show some traces of major controversies in the Latin American church on subjects such as how to evaluate the first evangelization and the Catholic stamp it imposed on culture, how to assess popular religion, and the modernization of culture.

II. Evangelization and inculturation of the gospel: a critical look at history

The theological and pastoral thinking we have seen expressed in documents from the bishops tends to regard inculturation as the church's response to the challenge of evangelizing culture. But this proposal is situated within a five-centuries-long history. As I have said, the subject of inculturation in Latin America inevitably leads to a critical review of the history of these five centuries of evangelization on the continent. This critical look is necessary, because it will shed more light on the successes and mistakes, the challenges and difficulties that lie along the course of inculturating the gospel in Latin America.

Evangelization and the origin of Latin America culture

We need to cast a critical look at this history also because – on a deep level – 'Latin American culture' itself (with its complexities, diversities and internal contradictions) is the product of a multifacetted process, one of whose force lines was the evangelization (or, to be more precise, the 'Christianization') of the native peoples. Others were the military conquest and political and economic colonization. In speaking of 'Latin American culture', I am not seeking to prejudge the issue by claiming a culture common to all peoples and social levels in Latin America nor an 'identity' or 'soul' shared in culture, nor a particular 'substrate' in it. I am referring simply to the undeniable fact that 'Latin America' became such as a result of the Iberian conquest and colonization of the sixteenth century.

Before this process, nothing like Latin America existed; in its place was a great multiplicity, dissimilarity and dispersion of peoples and cultures, many of which had no contact with one another. The European invasion brought about a 'foundational period' of a new economic, political and cultural entity. These are what some (the bishops' documents referred to, for example) have called an 'encounter'. It was certainly a most unequal or asymmetrical sort of encounter. The European side, obviously much the stronger in this process, determined the make-up of this new social and cultural entity, relatively homogenous and cohesive, not through its capacity for assimilating native cultures, but through levelling them to the ground. It mattered not at all whether they were dealing with cultures recently emerged from Neolithic times or highly complex and developed ones, well advanced in the arts and understanding of nature. At a stroke, they all became simply 'Indians': all had to be subdued militarily, all had to pay tribute and make economic contributions, all had to be made subjects of the crown and all had to become Christians and be baptized.

This process, which was, at one and the same time, the gestation and constitution of a new socio-cultural (colonial) entity and 'evangelization' ('Christianization'), left deep scars that have marked the relationship between 'evangelization' and 'culture' throughout the five centuries of the history of Latin America. Some points of particular importance for understanding the problems of inculturation at the present time can be picked out.

Evangelization and power

One of the aspects that emerges most clearly (and has been the object of many analyses and polemical arguments) is the conjunction between evangelizing mission, colonial political power and economic exploitation (of natural riches and the indigenous work force). Beyond the differences that obviously exist between the various roles (missionary, conquistador, colonial settler) and those that arose among the Spaniards themselves in the way they treated the Indians and regarded their status as human beings, there is no doubt that all these elements formed part of a whole: European expansion. Seen from the other side, that of the native peoples, who were suffering radical destruction, all these personages were first and foremost 'European', or, perhaps more accurately, the new 'masters'. Together with the death of their societies, their customs and freedoms, the Indians were experiencing the death of their gods.[1] A whole world was dying in the face of the implacable expansion of another that was overlaying it and rolling over it. And the missionaries were part of this world, just as much as the conquistadors, slave-owners or traders. In this way, evangelization reached these lands already laden with power – with a devastating power. This does not of course remove the importance of the great divide between those who proposed Christianization with the help of military and state coercion (under threat of 'just war', slavery and so on) and those who maintained that the only way of evangelizing the Indians was through peaceful and persuasive means.[2] Nevertheless, there is no denying the fact that, from the moment it became part of the constellation of European expansion, evangelization – or, more specifically, the Catholic Church – could not detach itself from power: a power that flattened and subjected, that consolidated a situation of extreme oppression and exploitation.

Nor did the church, in these five centuries, make too much effort to distance itself from power. Once its inner tensions and conflicts, provoked by the atrocities of the conquest in the sixteenth century, had passed, it assumed, with increasing naturalness and ease, its place as part of the power structure in society. In this way, being a missionary or a cleric meant sharing in this power; becoming a Christian, being initiated into the teaching and sacraments of the church, meant taking on the protection of this power. So from this 'foundational period' on, the church – and evangelization with it – placed itself unequivocally in a well-defined social and cultural 'setting', the side of the power groupings in society. From there it extended its influence to those without power: the poor and outcast. With allowances made for the inevitable and logical changes brought by history, the church has stayed in this social setting until now. In the internal conflict that has shaken it in the last decades (around the 'option for the poor', human rights, the base communities and liberation theology), this has remained one of the central factors. And now everything points to the fact that the neo-conservative trend supported by Rome is succeeding in reaffirming this historical characteristic of being a 'church close to the source of power'.

So we have to ask: is inculturation possible from these positions of power? And if it is possible, what characteristics will it have? The answers are not easy, particularly bearing in mind that what was being produced was precisely the foundation or gestation of a new society, based on the annihilation of the native societies and the political, economic and cultural expansion of Europe.

So, from one point of view, one can argue that there has, in effect, been a process of 'inculturation', to the extent that Christianity and the church have been major factors in the gestation of a new society and culture. But at the same time one would have to point out that this has not been an 'inculturation of the gospel', but rather the creation of a culture based on the influence of Iberian Christianity within that process. In this way a culture came into being whose religious axis was Catholicism, transplanted from the Iberian peninsular and implanted in the new territories. Still today there are those who think that the core element of 'Latin American culture' is its Catholic character.[3] But this transplant of European Christianity is far from being an 'inculturation'. Throughout all these five centuries, a whole brew of cultural expressions – including religious ones – unadapted to the official Catholicism has been boiling.

Such are the paradoxes of power. The huge colonial power proved effective in destroying societies and cultures, but very limited when it came to building relatively integrated social and cultural systems. Around the pole of official society and culture, a vast and heterogenous galaxy of cultures of the excluded (Indians, blacks and *mestizos*) built up, sharing only marginally in European culture. The Christianity of a 'church close to the sources of power' thereby showed its strong limitations in becoming inculturated in these peripheries.

Evangelization and human dignity

The society and culture that resulted from European-Christian expansion are deeply marked by dualism. This is not only a matter of the social and economic inequalities that appear virtually inevitably in all societies, but of exclusions that have come to take on an 'anthropological level'.

It is well known that the colonization of America gave rise to a debate that permeated the whole sixteenth century, the importance of which cannot be exaggerated: the controversy over the 'nature' of the Indians.[4] It was not so much surprise in the face of the unexpected, or ingenuousness, but rather concern to justify the practices of extermination and brutal exploitation, that led to the proposition of the 'theory' that the Indians were of a different nature from the Spaniards: animals or semi-animals, subhuman or 'natural slaves'. In this way, social and cultural differences took on an anthropological depth. All could not be equal, since not all were authentically human beings.

Although theoretically those who upheld the equality of Indians and Europeans, and therefore the fully human nature and dignity of the Indians (Bartolomé de Las Casas, Francisco de Vitoria), against those who maintained the thesis of natural slavery (led by Juan Ginés de Sepúlveda), carried the day, in practice something rather different happened. The outcome of the 'encounter' between European and indigenous cultures was a culture in which there were first-class (Europeans) and second-class (natives or blacks and, later, those of mixed race) people. These were in fact none other than the sub-human beings posited by the natural slavery theory: without dignity, deprived of virtually all rights, condemned to slavery from birth. Far from being eroded with time, this cultural feature was consolidated over the centuries and is still in place today (covered over with the cloak of formal-legal equality for all), applied not only to the native Americans but to the great majorities of those excluded from the first class. This is perhaps the most distinctive feature of 'Latin American culture': the denial of human dignity to the poor (the excluded); or, in other words, a culture that expresses the structural dualism of society as 'anthropological difference'.

What can 'inculturating the gospel' mean and imply in this culture? And, what happened in reality? There cannot be much doubt that the gospel would have led to a radical critique of this culture and to an inculturation among the excluded as a condition of upholding their human dignity. This is the route undertaken by Las Casas and certain other missionaries. But this route was blocked from the moment when evangelizing mission was placed within the greater constellation of European expansion.

From then on, the only part in which an 'inculturation' (more of European Christianity than of the gospel) could take place was the culture of the elite groups made up of those who were considered properly 'human'. 'Second-class' persons were the object of various mission strategies, which sought to baptize them and teach them Christian doctrine. But for the church, too, they remained 'second-class Christians'. Toward the excluded, the church, in the best of cases, developed attitudes of benevolent protectionism. But its greatest and best efforts were directed to serving and educating the ruling classes, and to influencing them. In the nineteenth century and more distinctly from the beginning of the twentieth century, these ruling classes began to distance themselves ideologically and culturally from the church. Then the weakness of the church's implantation in Latin America and its culture became obvious: church life has become increasingly dependent on 'overseas aid', for both personnel and finances.

Evangelization and culture

Has there then been no inculturation of the gospel in the cultures of the excluded and subordinated sectors of society (Indians, peasants, blacks, *mestizos* and the like)? A look at the church's attitude to cultures other than the European-Christian confirms the assessment that the 'Catholic' character attributed to traditional Latin American culture is not really a proof or indication of inculturation. There is no doubt that from the beginning missionaries made efforts not only to learn native languages, but to translate Christian doctrine into these languages; furthermore – though far more timidly and sporadically – efforts were made at adapting ritual to appeal to native cultures.[5] Nevertheless, overall, the predominant attitude was not merely a rejection of native cultures, but even a 'demonization' of them. For the missionaries, native cultures were often works of the devil (their religion was worship of the devil, their temples were constructions of the devil, their customs were inspired by the devil . . .). It is particularly striking to note that this judgment on native cultures was shared even by missionaries who were extremely harsh in their criticisms of the greed and abuses of the Spaniards.[6]

This judgment on native cultures (and the same applied to African cultures) removed the minimal foundations for advancing any 'inculturation' (although the concept was not disputed), since this supposes a basic openness to recognizing the presence of God in cultures, both in their cognitive and evaluative expressions ('seeds of the Word') and in their searches for meaning and their longings and hopes (the action of the 'Spirit').

The – later – relationship of the church with the varied forms of 'popular religion' and popular cultures on the continent can be seen in the same light. In the past few years, the official church has recognized – perhaps too late – the value and 'Catholic' character of popular religion. But this cannot hide the fact that the church has continually treated the manifestations of popular religion with suspicion and mistrust – and still does. One only has to read the documents produced by the bishops at Medellín, Puebla and Santo Domingo to realize that the church sees popular religion as an imperfect form of Christianity, a religion for the simple, threatened by superstitions, cosmic fatalisms, syncretisms, ethical *non-sequiturs* and so on. Despite this, it is increasingly valued – especially since Puebla – as a sort of religious raw material that can be 'purified' or 'evangelized' by bringing it closer to the true Christian meaning of the sacraments and to the truths of Catholicism.

The fact is, however, that this 'popular religion' is the closest Latin American Christianity has come to an 'inculturation of the gospel'. Seen in this way, one can say that if inculturation has taken place, it has done so more or less behind the back or on the fringes of the official church. The demonization of autochthonous cultures and later mistrust of popular religion are the religious expression of a more pervasive attitude: the rejection or repulsion by European culture of anything other than itself. Despite this, there has inevitably been 'cultural intermingling' (popular cultures), distinct from the European cultural pole and incapable of being integrated in it. Has this produced what might be called 'typically Latin American' culture? However this may be, the Latin American historical elites (in the colonial period, the nineteenth century and still today) have despised this 'typical' culture and have lived fascinated by whatever came out of European culture. This is why the ruling classes have been called cultural 'Herodians'. The church, as we have seen, has not kept apart from this Herodian mentality.

From the aspects examined in our look at the history of evangelization in Latin America, we can see that the question of 'inculturation' is closely tied to questions of ecclesiology. The limitations and failures in inculturation are seen to be conditioned by ecclesiological directions and choices: a church that uses the seat of power as the setting from which to evangelize, in a predominantly exclusive society, and one which radically devalues the cultural constructs of the excluded.

III. Latin America at the crossroads of modernization

Cultures are constantly changing, given that they are the creation and expression of living societies, which have continually to face up to and resolve new historical challenges. These changes, however, come faster and go deeper in certain periods. This is what has been happening in Latin America since the middle of this century.

The episcopal documents from Medellín, Puebla and Santo Domingo register the anxiety these changes are producing in the church. The traditional culture that sank its roots in the colonial past, in which the church saw its most solid base for exercising influence and which justified the description 'Catholic continent', is fast dissolving. But the bishops are not alone in seeing the implications of these changes. Obviously without episcopal fears, other sectors (intellectuals, politicians, businessmen) are appreciating them and – perhaps a little ingenuously – proclaiming their optimism with regard to them, heralding them as the beginnings of a new era in the history of the continent: Latin America is in a rapid process of modernization and – so the optimists allege – should modernize itself still more rapidly, as the means of solving the problems that have kept it in a state of underdevelopment, poverty and backwardness.

Modernization seems to have increased in pace over the last decade. In this century there have already been processes of modernization impelled by rapid urbanization (as a result of the crisis or exhaustion of traditional agriculture) leading to vast and chaotic growth of cities, by 'developmentalist' policies, by the processes of industrialization and by the extension of education. But in the last few years the continent has entered on a new phase of modernization, and at a fresh pace: this is, paradoxically, the result of the crisis of the previous process of modernization, built on an 'economic model' known as 'developmentalist'. This model fell apart both economically and politically in the 1970s and 1980s, culminating in the external debt crisis and calling the whole idea of the state and the party system into question. Latin America has now been obliged to rethink its insertion in a 'new international economic order', forced to make internal economic and political 'structural adjustments': this is the new 'modernization' of economics and politics and it both requires and inevitably entails a modernization of culture.

Despite the fact that this new process of modernization grew out of the demise of the earlier one, both have something very definite in common: in both cases Latin America has been compelled (not by physical violence, but by that of deep crises) to modernize itself in accordance with the demands made by an order external to it (with its centre of gravity in the wealthy nations).

This comparison can also help to a better understanding of one important aspect of the historical and cultural development of Latin America. Just as it was formed into a relatively homogenous entity, from a wide diversity of indigenous cultures, by the European invasion in the sixteenth century, so the impacts of and coercion stemming from this European/Western pole have marked the decisive turning-points and provided the basic impulses in its history and culture.[7] The first impact was that of colonization, in which, even if it cannot properly be called 'modernization',[8] the social and cultural bases that were to lead to the coupling to later modernizing impulses were laid down. After this first impact, Latin America experienced another in the nineteenth century, leading to the wars of independence and the establishment of nation states, the importation of ideas deriving from the Enlightenment, and integration into the international market led by England. A third impact was the one crystallized in the developmentalist model from the mid-twentieth century and which, once again, was much more than an economic agenda: it was an attempt to apply the ideal of modern industrial society to the continent. When this impulse was exhausted and ended in failure, in the 1970s and 1980s, a new form of coercion appeared in the 1990s, urging modernization by new methods. This is based on the globalization and trans-nationalization of the world economy, the spread of communications and new information technology.

This shows that 'modernization' is not something so unusual in our cultural history (while accepting its new features today) and that at crucial moments in the past Latin America has experienced modernizing impulses more as a fate imposed from outside than as a development based on its own inner historical logic. It would in any case be a big mistake to assume that these external impulses have succeeded only in applying a superficial varnish of modernization to Latin American culture, beneath which lies a latent or sleeping 'soul', more its own, containing the religious fibres impressed by the first evangelization. This is not the case. By continual shoving, sometimes stumbling, the coercion emanating from the Western world and its culture has progressively penetrated and changed Latin American culture in the direction of modernization. At the same time, this is a modernization with its own proper Latin American features, not a simple reproduction or reflection of North American or European culture.

In its present phase, this coercion seems to be producing an exaggerated over-valuation of market forces and their extension to all spheres of social life, as well as of profit, private initiative and economic efficiency as criteria of the new modernization. On the other hand, however, this modernization has not produced changes in the authoritarian culture of politics, nor with regard to the discrimination suffered by the excluded sectors of the population. On the contrary: the modernization of the economy seems to be aggravating exclusions; this has its cultural counterpart in the reinforcement of discrimination and denial of human dignity to the excluded sectors of society. So, as applied to Latin America, the process can be called 'modernization without modernity'.[9]

There are, therefore, at the present time, powerful forces working towards a relative cultural homogenization in a 'mass culture', based on mercantile models and the growing influence of mass communications media. But there are also powerful forces – from the excluded sectors – working to reproduce on a larger scale cultural heterogeneity between the transnational culture of the elites and the multiple cultures of those excluded from it.

The processes of modernization of culture in the second half of this century have created a new context for evangelization. What seems to concern the church most is the rapid dissolution of traditional peasant culture and its Catholic 'popular religion'. What we are looking at, however, is not a steamrolling invasion by secularization. The ruling classes have become secularized to a large extent, but Latin American modernization has not quenched religious longings and needs in other sectors – particularly among the excluded. Their needs, however, are not being channelled into Catholicism, but into a vigorous flourishing of autochthonous evangelical (Pentecostal) churches, sects, spiritist and healing cults and the like.

In this new situation, inculturation of the gospel cannot hope to create a new 'Christian' (or Catholic) culture. Such a turning back is not possible, nor is it desirable in view of the limitations of the first evangelization. Evangelization of culture in Latin America has to be consistent with the 'option for the poor' expressed by the Latin American church. This option has been the fruit of a deep process of evangelical renewal in the church – or, more precisely, in some sectors of it. It has laid the foundations for undertaking evangelization from a fresh vantage point, with the church distancing itself, in the first place, from the apparent advantages of its close relationship with the centres of power and the culture of the elites, and seeking rather to inculturate the gospel in the varied cultures of excluded groups. The gospel speaks to these cultures of the human dignity, as 'children of God', of those who are excluded from society and discriminated against by it: the poor of the shanty-towns and remote rural areas, the Indians and blacks. In this way, inculturation would be seeking to transform a feature that, as we have seen, has been such a strong characteristic of the culture of the continent. This can lead, finally, to a positive revaluation of these cultures and allow the reaffirmation of these cultural identities as sources of criticism of the 'cultural modernization' that is now looking so one-dimensional. It is, though, obviously not a case of trying to put the brakes on modernization through evangelization. Latin America – and this means all sectors of its society – has to take on the challenges of modernization. But inculturation of the gospel in the cultures of the excluded can help – unlike in the past – to make this confrontation with Western culture more critical and creative.

The subject of inculturation thereby points once more to ecclesiological questions: it means the church must make particular choices and follow particular lines of action. It is clear that, at present, the church of Latin America is deeply divided on these points. The future of evangelization of culture in Latin America depends on the way these conflicts are resolved.

Translated by Paul Burns

Notes

1. Cf. O. Beozzo, 'Visão indígena da conquista e da evangelização', in *Inculturação e libertação*, CNBB/CIMI, São Paulo 1986, 79–104.
2. Cf. G. Gutiérrez, *En busca de los pobres de Jesucristo. El pensamiento de Bartolomé de Las Casas*, Lima 1992, 221–67. ET *Las Casas: In Search of the Poor of Jesus Christ*, Maryknoll, NY 1993.
3. John Paul II himself seems to credit Catholicism with being a unifying element in Latin America culture and identity, Inaugural Discourse at Santo Domingo, nn. 12, 24.
4. Cf. L. Hanke, *La humanidad es una*, Mexico City ²1985, 23–97.
5. Cf. R. Foerster, 'La acción evangelizadora de la Compañia de Jesús entre los mapuches de Chile', in G. Arroyo, J. Silva, F. Verdugo (eds.), *Por los caminos de América . . . Desafíos socio-culturales de la Nueva Evangelización*, Santiago 1992, 97–110.
6. Such was the case with Fray Toribio de Benavente (Motolinia). See his *Historia de los Indios de la Nueva España* (1541), Tratado I, chs II, III and IV, Madrid.
7. J. Comblin has said that the history of culture in Latin America is marked by three invasions of Western culture: that of the conquest, that of the nineteenth century, and that of the mid twentieth century. J. Comblin, *Reconciliación y liberación*, Santiago 1987, 240. See also L. Boff, *A New Evangelization*, Maryknoll, NY (*Good News to the Poor*, Tunbridge Wells) 1992, 16–18.
8. However, T. Todorov finds 'modern' features already in Cortés and the other Spanish conquistadors. *El problema del otro*, Mexico City 1987, 154–5.
9. Cf. N. Lechuer, *¿Son compatibles modernidad y modernización? El desafío de la democracia Latinoamericana* (FLASCO working document), Santiago 1990.

Evangelization and Youth Culture seen from French Canada

Jean-Guy Nadeau

'It's hell.' This expression illustrates the distance between youth culture and church culture. For young Québécois, what for the church is a place of damnation and intense pain, and consequently denotes situations of extreme suffering, is a description of conditions of amusement and intense pleasure. To say 'it's hell' indicates how much one enjoys something. 'It will be hell', says an announcement for a trip or some other activity which must not be missed. The title of one of our most lively and most-watched television shows proclaims joyfully, 'Hell is the rest of us'. Certainly these young people are skilled at modifying and reversing the meaning of the words of their elders, but what is remarkable here is the number of young people ignorant of the religious origin of this expression.

I shall be returning to this gap between youth culture and church culture. But since knowledge of the other is one of the first stages of evangelization, first of all I shall present some features of youth culture.

I. The dramatic social situation of young people

Since I cannot describe the different youth cultures here, some of which are better integrated into adult culture than others, I shall simply point out some general features in the more dramatic of them. In addition to the well-documented problems of young people's physical and emotional growth there are the problems relating to their social situation. If in their eyes their situation has never been an enviable one, we can well believe that its drama is increased by the fact that they live in a 'credit-card society'. How can anyone accept preparing for his or her future and sacrificing the present for it when all around, the whole of society is living on credit, and both the celebrities of this society and its media emphasize that the future is limited or at least mortgaged? How can anyone accept living for the future when we are told that its resources will be serving to pay for the present? And then there is amazement that young people think of the present moment! I may have been able to grow up with an awareness that later I would have a recognized place in society and a role to play in its development, but things are different for young people today. Why go to school? 'Dad,' my thirteen-year-old daughter is already asking me, 'Will there be work for us later, or am I studying for nothing?'

If these young people suffer over their future, they also suffer over the present. They cannot find a place in our society where they feel noticed, and often come to feel that they are useless beings, second-class citizens, even troublemakers. Moving from childhood to adulthood, they find that little importance is attached to their present: 'Wait your turn', 'Youth must pass.' Young people also suffer the absence of recognition in our society of what they have to say. Certainly they were not much listened to in former societies, but that did not have the same consequences, since adolescence was very much shorter and these societies did not have the same democratic pretensions as ours. If little importance is attached in our society to what young people have to say, this is certainly because in it they do not have the authority given by social and family responsibilities; but it is also because what they say often shocks us. Young people are absolute, blunt, and see and talk about the world only from a vision of things that we find very limited. But how could it be otherwise?

Very often our relationships with young people are lived out only under the mode of confrontation, in a dialogue of the deaf, or one in which the other's word is discredited from the start. Michel de Certeau identified education as a struggle to the death between two partners, one defending an identity which has been acquired and laboriously constructed, the other his or her right to exist.[1] Young people are defending their right to live in the present and their right to explore its possibilities, their right to determine their existence themselves. But it is as though they had always to justify their being, whereas that of adults is regarded as having been acquired, as a matter of course.

Finally, it is said that young people do not believe in anything. But in what and whom could they believe, in the situation in which they find themselves? Many of them, deeply wounded by life, cannot believe in adults, in life, in God. 'You know what you can do with your God of love . . .' In a recent study,[2] Jacques Grand'Maison speaks of the spiritual drama of adolescents. This drama is not primarily that they do not believe in God or in Jesus Christ, but that they do not even believe in themselves and their possibilities for the future, or in the other, or in their society, and sometimes even in life.

A deteriorating situation

Even if young Canadians are privileged compared with youth in other parts of the world, there are some indications of a deterioration in their situation. The most eloquent is certainly the suicide rate, which is the main cause of death after road accidents among young Québécois. Then there is unemployment, a social death which affects more than forty per cent of young workers, while the great majority of jobs available are only precarious, or dead-end jobs. Another indication is the level of pregnancy among minors. In 1990, fourteen per cent of girls of less than twenty-one had had a pregnancy before the age of seventeen. Despite widespread programmes of information, like AIDS campaigns, in 1992 there were twice as many cases of pregnancy among those under seventeen than in 1985. Finally, there is also an alarming rise among young people in violence that they have been in the forefront of experiencing,[3] both at school and in the streets.

All observers are agreed that the young American Indians are far worse off than their peers. The suicide, alcoholism, unemployment, violence, imprisonment rates are much higher, and sum up almost everything the media tell us about this youth.

American Indians or not, the image of youth which the media offer to both young people and adults is largely negative. And numerous articles in the daily press bear witness to the violence of youth. A Québécois woman's magazine with a very high circulation and a reasonable price (*Chatêlaine*) entitled its May 1993 number *The Capsized Generation*. 'They steal, they fight, they terrify.' The table of contents reads like this. 'The Capsized Generation – Your Shirt or Your Life! – My Daughter is a Neo-Nazi – I'm Afraid of My Son – Dad, I'm Taking You to Court – How Have the Youth Got Here? – I Hate My Father.'[4]

We can understand why young people protest against the treatment given to them by our media. And yet, there are riches among them, positive achievements of which the media hardly speak. But it is only by direct experience or by word of mouth that one can get to know of some fantastic projects, even if those responsible for them have sent press releases and invitations to the media. The media convey in the face of the future a fatalism which does nothing to support young people's taste for life. It is as if we had nothing to offer them but the disillusionment of our dreams as 'baby boomers', as fatal choices made by our society. And yet young people want to live, to believe in the future. 'Stop cramming pessimism down our throats', cried one of them in an open letter to *La Presse* of Montreal.

II. Young people at a distance: the gospel and the church

Given this dramatic situation, above all if one also takes into account the values that young people profess like justice and authenticity, one could believe that they would be particularly open to a gospel which proclaims blessings for the poor, those who weep, those who thirst for justice and peace. In preaching and incarnating the gospel of God's interest in a proximity to those excluded from religion and respectable society, was not Jesus better received by the outcast than the well-to-do, by those without religion than the religious? If we are still announcing good news, how is it that young people are not interested in it?

A first factor: secularity and religious indifference

Clearly a first reason relates to the secularity of our culture. I happen to believe that Jesus' task of evangelization was easier than ours. At least he was addressing a culture for which God made some sense. If Jesus' activity could restore a place to the poor of his time and give meaning to their lives by creating a positive context for them in the sight of God, it was because a relationship with God was recognized by their culture. In it religion was politics, and defined the city. Things are different today, now that the city is defined on quite a different basis and religious faith is thought negligible. The positivism of our culture is an obstacle to the recognition of a God whom one cannot see and cannot measure, who does not do anything visible. 'I will believe in God when he does something for me,' said a young man in an interview.

Even if some young people in some respects reject this positivist and egocentric mentality, they are steeped in this culture which from the point of view of a believer is characterized by religious indifference. This is not primarily the indifference of individuals but above all that of cultural symbols, the symbols which shape mentalities and determine the horizon of the world, the horizon of the meaning of a society.

A second factor: the gap between youth culture and church culture

A second reason for the lack of interest in the gospel among young people relates to the inculturation of faith in what I shall describe as church culture. The proclamation of the gospel is never simple, but is always proclamation of a gospel inculturated in the church. Now there would seem to be an enormous difference between this culture and that of young people, and one can ask if young people are not more strangers to the church than to the gospel.

At the risk of generalizing it can be said that young people today live in what one could call rock culture: a culture in which everything passes, everything is 'flash', event, sensations, heightened emotions. For many of them rock is a force, an experience of power, the place where they cry out their lives. In the paroxysm of decibels, in the clamour of guitars and the singer, which is echoed in the energy of extended fists, rock is not only a place of sensation but of an expression of rage, anguish and anxiety, a place of purging. It can be the occasion of turning in on oneself, but it can also be an experience of transcendence and even communion. The rock spectacles, the religious character of which their chroniclers often report, are like a ritual in which people explore the chaos of an ill-assured identity, in which they break up the rigidity of a concrete society, in which the tumult of sensations make them forget both the past and concern for the future, in which they also have communion with something greater than themselves.

The Sunday tam-tams

So no one should think that young people find rituals repugnant, even if they avoid ours, which they find very boring. They choose theirs, in their image. For example, the young people of Montreal and surrounding areas have produced a new Sunday ritual, spontaneous and uncontrolled. In the middle of the city, at the foot of Mont-Royal, thousands of them gather each Sunday to vibrate, dance, smoke and let off steam to the sound of the tam-tams of Black Africa and the Maghreb, South America, Quebec and elsewhere. Over the years 'the tam-tams' have become a place of exploration, encounter, fraternization and a rare ethnic conviviality.

'A tranquil church in a volcanic society'

This culture is remote from a church culture in which everything seems to young people to be controlled, or very hard and repetitive, a culture which leaves little room for sensations and movement – apart from that of the liturgical cycle or the priest walking composedly to the altar. Although I am no longer twenty, I too get bored with our liturgical celebrations, where church culture is most manifest, though its expression is still freest there. Finally, ecclesiastical sedimentation, particularly in its codifications of dogmas and prohibitions, is far removed from the experimentation which characterizes young people.

In 1978 Jacques Grand'Maison described our church as 'a tranquil church in a volcanic society'. This image well describes the gap between youth culture and church culture, a gap which does not make the evangelization of young people at all easy. At least Jesus participated in the same culture as those whom he addressed. On a world scale, U2 is one of the most popular rock groups, and identifies itself as a Christian group. But how many of us have the cultural sensitivity to recognize the religious dimension of their music, not to say a prayer in a guitar solo?[5]

One of the dramas of evangelization is that young people identify the gospel with a church which they consider static, arrested, authoritarian, one institution among others but without relevance. In fact, they see it as a million miles from what interests them, what is significant for them. It is painful to have to acknowledge that despite all our efforts, or for lack of them, the church that young people know bars access to the gospel rather than facilitating it. This is a normal situation to the degree that young people reject every institution, but all the same it makes us ask questions about the image projected by our church, which is institutional rather than evangelical.

III. Evangelization and the evangelization of young people

Youth pastoral work and recognition of Jesus Christ

Some people certainly have positive relations with church people . . . and are often surprised that such people belong to the church. In a revealing way, young people will say that they are 'OK' *even if* they are priests, religious or Christians. But these relations rarely go beyond the personal dimension, and hardly lead to the gospel or the church community. In a study on pastoral workers who are recognized as significant both by young people and the ecclesial community, Mitsi Leduc notes that of the young people who frequent with these workers, very few, despite everything, come to recognize and to speak of Jesus Christ.[6] Does Jesus remain attached to the world of naive childhood, as Grand'Maison's research indicates, or still to the ecclesial institution? What, in one case or the other, alienates young people?

The role of these pastoral workers in the growth of young people is inestimable wherever young people are given support in developing faith in themselves, in others and in the future. But such apprenticeship in life cannot be identified with evangelization, even if it is a major dimension of it. Can one speak of evangelization without an explicit proclamation and reception of Jesus Christ? People sometimes refer to 'Matthew 25' to affirm that the explicit proclamation and recognition of Jesus Christ are not what matters, but rather that the hungry should be fed, strangers welcomed, the sick and prisoners visited, the littlest ones cared for, and that justice should reign. Although that is necessary for the life of the gospel, 'Matthew 25' proposes more: not only an ethic but the recognition of God and of Jesus Christ.

It is in the character of evangelistic practices to be practices of revelation, at least 'disclosure situations', i.e. not only to be concerned for the world but to project a world in which another relates to us.[7] If the practices of Matthew 25. 31–46 are far from being insignificant in themselves, the judgment of the Son of man reveals their profound nature. In putting them within the horizon of faith, he does the work of revelation, through and beyond ethics, social service and humanism.

Practices in the evangelization of young people favoured today

Catholic religious teaching in public schools is the mode of evangelizing young people most favoured by the Catholic church here. Even if the majority of Québécois youth have undergone eleven years of religious teaching, most observers are agreed in saying that in practice they are ignorant of the whole of Christian faith, apart from a morality which they sum up either under prohibitions or 'love one another'. What is said in the Bible or the Gospels, of whose dramas they know little, seems to them to be children's stories.

To complement this public teaching, our church has invested the major part of its personnel and resources in the sacramental initiation of children and their preparatory catechesis. Here we have to accept that initiation has proved to have no effect on existence.

However, there is awareness of the importance of initiation for a human group as well as for the one initiated, who acquires a new status in it with his or her rights and responsibilities. Rites of initiation are a cruel gap in our society, from which they are virtually absent, and in our church, where they are ineffective in practice. Certainly young people invite rites of initiation among peers, but these rites are not recognized in any way by society as a whole. The same goes for the church, where certain youth pastoral workers have invented very interesting rites of initiation which have been well received by young people, but still have not been recognized by the church.

The church continues to inspire numerous youth movements which prove to be among the most fertile areas of initiation into life and sometimes evangelization. By meeting adults who believe in them and listen to them, young people (as they say) here discover their value, find occasions for commitment and for learning the values of the gospel, and have an experience of openness to the other and to society. Contrary to the cultural current, here they have the experience of a group for which faith is living and significant. But these movements interest only a tiny minority of young people.

Some demands made by the evangelization of young people
Evangelization proceeds by the clarification of crucial issues in life, the announcement of the newness of the gospel, the search for fundamental convergences between life and the gospel, a critique of cultural, economic and political contradictions which prevent liberation and development, and the invention of new modes of being, thinking, acting and living together. This takes place on the basis of a daily companionship, a steeping in the natural places of the culture to be evangelized.[8]

Some qualities, though unequal ones, further this process among young people: energy and a taste for living, a critical sense, the quest for a meaning in life, solidarity with the outcast, a concern for the dignity of people, the need to believe in the possibility of a new start and thus of forgiveness, getting back on the rails, etc. Despite our culture, young people manifest a degree of openness to the religious.[9] But this is a vague sense of the religious, which is difficult to name and resists any identification from outside. Young people firmly refuse to accept an already codified religious meaning for their experience, above all a Christian meaning. I make no excuse for repeating, since it is so important, that for them Jesus and his God are childish things, out of date, insignificant. Besides, while the institutional image of the church may close some doors to evangelization, others are perhaps opening between young people and a church which is stalling, losing prestige and social relevance; between young people and Christians who love life and commit themselves to the service of the world. A sixty-year-old priest who gives food and clothing to young people living in the streets whom they know under the name of Pops, affirms, 'I never speak formally of God to young people. But I have a certain meaning: "Pops", a father. And perhaps God is a little like that, or Pops is a little like God.'

Taking up the openness of *Gaudium et spes* to sharing the joys and hopes, the sadness and the anguish, of people of this time, Pedro Arupe considered experiential assimilation to the life-style of groups with which one has to work as the first stage of evangelization. That applies to the evangelization of young people, which goes by way of sharing their experience and their culture, listening, engaging in dialogue and being patient, free companionship and the realization of plans, the proclamation of Jesus Christ first through the witness of life, reciprocity and the quest of the Other, and in the development of the expressions of this quest. This is, and will be, the price of the church's evangelization, and at the same time the church will be evangelized by the newness of the gospel.

What must be offered through this companionship with young people is not a ready-made meaning, codified in a particular language or culture which they have simply to adopt and then adapt, but encounter with believers and, through them, with Jesus Christ, a meaning to elaborate in the light of Christ and the gospel. Evangelization will be not so much the effort to transmit a message as a contribution towards establishing a different way of living out social relationships, marked by a horizon of faith. It will be not so much the effort to transmit a Christian or ecclesial culture with its secular expressions as to offer a horizon of particular transcendence. For us, it will be the possibility of a saving encounter with God through the recognition of Jesus Christ and the other.

Finally, young people hold us to the authenticity of what we propose. If only out of a lack of interest, sometimes stamped with scorn for Christianity, they always question the coherence of our life with what we say about faith. This coherence is beyond question the greatest challenge of evangelization. With love of life and service, it constitutes one of the major features of believers which the young people who affirm their faith claim to have found on their way.

Translated by John Bowden

Notes

1. M. de Certeau, *L'étranger ou l'union dans la différence*, Paris 1969.
2. J. Grand'Maison (ed.), *Le drame spirituel des adolescents*, Cahiers d'études pastorales 10, Montreal 1992.
3. Between 25% and 33% of them will have been sexually abused during childhood, without counting other forms of injury.
4. The fact that this issue is interspersed with advertisements for perfumes and beauty products, and followed by articles on decoration, fashion, tourism and cooking, seems to me to reveal a social function of these adult interests which includes those of

the 'home' denounced by E. McDonagh, 'Man and Woman are in the Image of God and We Are All Brothers and Sisters in Christ', *Concilium* 130, 1979, 115–24. If that is the meaning of the life that we offer to young people, should we be surprised at their own 'entertainment' and the way in which so many drop out? We say we regret this, but do we really want them to change our world?

5. 'Edge's guitar solo in "Love is Blindness" is a more eloquent prayer than anything I could write', affirms Bono, the leader of the group (*Musician* 178, August 1993, 36).

6. M. Leduc, *Pour une animation pastorale signifiante auprès des jeunes*, Montreal 1993.

7. J.-G. Nadeau, 'La fonction révélante des pratique pastorales', in B. Reymond (ed.), *La théologie pratique d'expression française aujourd'hui*, Paris 1993.

8. J. Grand'Maison, *La seconde evangélisation, 2.1, Outils majeurs*, Héritage et projet 2, Montreal 1973.

9. As witnessed also by the evening prayer, above all a cry of distress which some address to a supreme being – or to their dead grandparents.

III · Recent Discussion

Two Question Marks: Inculturation and Multiculturalism

Gregory Baum

Some categories employed in theology and the social sciences tend to disguise rather than reveal the concrete historical reality. To these categories, it seems to me, belong inculturation and multiculturalism.

The question of inculturation

The ecclesiastical literature on inculturation, including beautiful texts found in a series of Vatican documents, presuppose without any investigation that Catholicism is an ensemble of religious truths and ritual practices that can become incarnate in any culture whatever. It is one thing to say that the gospel or the proclamation of Jesus Christ can be communicated to any culture, live in it, transform it and achieve in it a new and rich expression. It is quite another to say the same thing of Catholicism. My concern here is not whether the gospel can find authentic expression in the world's diverse cultures. What I wish to question is that Catholicism is capable of such incarnations.

Catholicism is a particular embodiment of the gospel of Jesus Christ. Catholicism is a religious culture. It is flexible, it exists in a variety of countries representing different cultures, it has acquired slightly different faces in various parts of the world. Still, the self-organization of Catholicism, the concepts, ideals and practices of governance, constitute an ecclesiastical culture. This culture is not taken from the world in which the New Testament was written; it is derived, rather, from the Catholic Church's experience in subsequent centuries, from the needs of local and regional churches, the concern for the universal church and the organizational forms existing in society at large. According to Catholic teaching, this institutional development has been sparked by initiatives taken in New Testament times and subsequently shaped and guided by the Holy Spirit. Because the Catholic religion sees itself as founded upon scripture and tradition, Catholicism is a religious culture.

Sociologists often define a culture as an ensemble of customs, laws, values and rituals that defines a community's collective identity and determines the interaction of the members among themselves. The point I wish to make here is that not only sociologists regard Catholicism as a culture, but the church itself, recognizing its Spirit-guided self-unfolding over the centuries, regards itself as a culture. Catholicism sees itself as the incarnation of the gospel in a particular ecclesiastical form.

But if Catholicism itself is a culture, how can it be 'inculturated' in the diverse cultural traditions of the world? The literature on inculturation tends to disguise this question.

To illustrate this point I wish to show that Catholicism has been unable to inculturate itself in modern, Western democratic societies. The ethic of governance proper to the Catholic Church is at odds with the correspond- ing ethic of the Western democracies. However corrupt these democracies may be, they share certain ideals and values; and the people in these democracies make ethical judgments on the actual performance of their governments in terms of these ideals and values. They demand, for instance, accountability and transparency. Objecting to traditional aristo- cratic or contemporary authoritarian forms of governance, people in democracies demand that those who govern justify their decisions in rational terms, name the persons and agencies that have been consulted, and reveal the process by which the decisions have been reached. Unless there are good and urgent reasons for it, people regard secrecy as unethical.

To give another example, let me mention the demand of contemporary ethics that people accused of irregularities or crimes have a right to due process. This demands the separation of the legislative and judicial powers or, more concretely, the existence of independent courts. The denial of due process and the absence of the appropriate institutions – in the church and in authoritarian states – is regarded by people in democratic cultures as unethical.

Catholicism as an ecclesiastical culture has not been able to incarnate itself in the modern, Western democracies. The church's ethic of governance presupposes the division between *'maiores'* and *'minores'*, between a higher group of men who make the laws and determine policy, and a lower group, the great majority, whose task is to obey, to whom the governing body is not accountable, who have no right to demand transparency, and who have no access to independent courts that protect them from injustices inflicted on them by members of the higher group. As a consequence, Catholicism as an ecclesiastical culture appears not only as a foreign institution in the modern Western democracies but as unethical, as the incarnation of an ethic of governance that has become unacceptable.

I add to this that because of the sinister role played by unquestioning obedience in Fascism and Communism, citizens in democratic cultures have a revulsion against any system that demands unquestioning obedience. After the practice of obedience in Fascist and Communist parties, the traditional Catholic concept of obedience seems no longer acceptable. There is a qualitative difference between obedience to God and obedience to human beings, however exalted. It is not surprising, therefore, that in democratic cultures, many bishops and superiors of religious orders have introduced a dialogue structure in the exercise of their authority. What is emerging here is a new dynamics between decision-makers and the members of their communities. But since the relation of bishops and their regional churches to Rome is still determined by the traditional, vertical, non-dialogical practice of suprement authority, the foreign-looking, ecclesiastical culture, mitigated by progressive bishops, remains intact.

Discussing possible inculturations of Catholicism, it is therefore necessary to examine to what extent Catholicism itself is a culture. Perhaps 'inculturation' is an ideal that has little foundation in reality. Conservative Catholics have a strong argument when they say that Catholicism is an ecclesiastical and spiritual culture, a specifically European creation combining the scriptural witness and classical humanism, which is embodied in the art and architecture of the élite as well as the customs and feasts of the populus, which is ruled by high-minded leaders standing above the fashions of the day, capable of communicating this great tradition to all who wish to join it from whatever background.

The question of multiculturalism

A few years ago the Canadian government adopted a policy of multiculturalism and created a ministry of the same name.[1] Responding to the recent immigration of people from all parts of the globe and affirming the liberal ideal of equal opportunity, the government proposed the controversial idea that Canadian society is being constituted by many cultures, that there exists no receiving culture in which the cultures of immigrants (and of the Native peoples) are situated, and that Canada is therefore multi-cultural, allowing each citizen to live in his or her own cultural environment, none of which enjoys a privileged status. Canada, according to the phrase used, is bilingual (English and French) and multicultural.

In the largely francophone province of Quebec, which enjoys a certain autonomy within the Canadian confederation, the theory of multiculturalism has not been accepted.[2] Instead, the provincial government recognizes the francophone host culture of Quebec, which receives the various immigrant cultures. Quebec has called this the policy of convergence: its aim is not the assimilation of immigrant or Native peoples but rather to foster a process of convergence by which the host culture, learning from the minorities, experiences a certain transformation, and where the minority cultures reconciled to their new environment also undergo significant changes. A gradual convergence of this kind should make it possible to articulate a series of common public values.

Quite recently the Canadian government, worried about the disintegration of society, has given up the multicultural discourse, even though the appropriate ministry has not been renamed.[3] Nor has the government made clear what precisely its new policy will be.

In my opinion, the category of multiculturalism disguises rather than reveals the social reality of modern society. To understand this complex cultural pattern of modern society I wish to distinguish between what some sociologists call primary and secondary cultures. Primary culture refers to the home environment in which the child is born, including language, food, customs and the relations to parents and other members of the family as well as the relations of these among themselves. In traditional societies the primary culture often stretches out into the street and the village and determines a wide sector of the public culture, including its songs, its literature and its wisdom tradition. But such an extension is hardly possible in modern society, not only because the street has become pluralistic and people with diverse primary cultures populate the same town, but also because there exists a powerful secondary culture that shapes people's lives, dreams and aspirations.

Secondary culture refers to the ideas, values and practices promoted by the major institutions of modern society, especially the capitalist market, technology, the mass media and democratic institutions.

This secondary culture is very powerful. Capitalism and technology shape the values and practices of the entire population, including the recent immigrants, even if they have arrived from pre-industrial or formerly socialist societies. The work ethic, competition, upward mobility and self-promotion are quickly learnt, even if the primary culture prevents these values from entering the home. Television advertising produces a yearning for more leisure, greater comfort and the enjoyment of more consumer goods. Technology teaches people that they have control over their environment, that their lives can be made easier by mechanical instruments, and even that instrumental rationality is the safest guide in solving personal and social problems. The market system, moreover, defines people's location in society, their freedom and their slavery.

The multicultural discourse disguises the power of assimilation exercised by the major institutions in society. Secondary culture is so powerful that it invades the home and undermines the primary cultures to which people have been deeply attached. What is taking place in modern society – I am thinking especially of North America, including French-speaking Quebec – is what some sociologists call 'deculturation', the destruction of primary cultures and the creation of a cultural emptiness in the home that is communicated to children and prevents them from acquiring spiritual or non-utilitarian values.

On the positive side we note that part of secondary culture are the institutions of democracy that generate values and aspirations affecting the immigrant communities, creating the desire to participate in society and prompting them to set up social and political organizations to foster their interests and defend their rights. The Canadian experience has shown that for the majority of immigrants the process of democratic assimilation is rapid. Immigrant groups learn very quickly to create community organizations to defend their rights and their honour against the prejudice and discrimination inflicted upon them in society. At the same time the assimilation of democratic values tends to question their life in the home, often still defined by fixed patterns of authority.

The power of assimilation exercised by the secondary culture is very strong. Even the Native people with their age-old cultural tradition find that as they wrestle against Canadian society to preserve their collective identity, they have to study law, argue in the courts, become clever in the use of the dominant idiom and turn to technology to create a system of communication of their own. It is a paradox (and a tragedy) that wrestling against modern industrial society easily becomes a modernizing process.

The notion of multiculturalism makes invisible the complex dynamics of modern society with its pluriformity of primary cultures, its class divisions, the individualism fostered by the market system, the desire for happiness through consumption fostered by the mass media, and the integrating effects of democratic practices and institutions. Threatened by the dominant (secondary) culture, the primary cultures create their own institutions to protect and foster the inherited community values –their parish or religious organization, their associations, clubs, stores, restaurants, book stores, theatres, etc. What emerge here are technically speaking subcultures – subcultures, I would add, that sustain the well-being of society as a whole and hence deserve its support. Yet in most cases these subcultures willingly fit themselves into the dominant culture defined by capitalism and technology.

The government of Quebec, as mentioned above, has rejected the concept of multiculturalism and instead taken up the policy of convergence. This policy recognizes that there are many forces that pull society apart – the widening economic gap, the growth of unemployment, the plurality of ethnic, religious and cultural background, and the prejudice and discrimination inflicted upon the minorities. But the same policy also recognizes the forces that integrate society – a public language, the legal system, democratic practices, human rights and the respect for pluri-ethnicity and multiple primary cultures, and the interdependence (even if distorted) of people created by the market system. While the policy of convergence wants to strengthen the forces that integrate society, it does not aim at the assimilation of immigrant groups (or Native peoples). In this context even the word integration is not useful. Convergence aims at the ongoing transformation of both, the receiving culture and the multiple primary cultures struggling for recognition. A good image of convergence is the transformation of people's food habits in modern society: while each ethnic group retains its own cuisine with additions from the mainstream, the host culture is enriched in its diet by dishes brought by the immigrants. The challenge is to pursue this policy of convergence so that it becomes possible to articulate common public values in the midst of ethnic and cultural pluralism.

Notes

1. *Multiculturalism . . . Being Canadian/Le multiculturalisme . . . être canadien*, Ministry of Supply and Services/Le ministère des approvisionnements et services, Ottawa, Canada 1987.

2. *La politique québecoise du développement culturelle*, 2 volumes, Gouvernment du Québec, Editeur officiel, Québec 1978.

3. *The Question of Immigration/La question de l'immigration*, and *Strategies of Integrating the Immigrants/Stratégies d'intégration des immigrants*, Ministry of Employment and Immigration/Le ministère de l'emploi et de l'immigration, Ottawa 1993.

A Confused Mission Scenario: A Critical Analysis of Recent Church Documents and Tendencies

Paulo Suess

A grey mist lies over the mission scene. All over the world new zeal is being combined with old methods. New forms of expression go hand in hand with fashionable design changes. The various discussions are confused, both in themselves and in relation to missionary praxis.

The resolutions of the Fourth General Assembly of the Latin American bishops in Santo Domingo (SD), the mission encyclical *Redemptoris missio* (RM) and other recent documents of the local and universal magisterium emphatically point to the 'missionary nature' of the church which was emphasized by Vatican II (*Ad gentes* 2, SD 12, RM 1). The same documents insist on the communication of this 'missionary nature' in missiology, which is to be included among the regular disciplines of theology. Missiology must demonstrate not only the specific relevance of all theological tractates to mission but above all also give a place to the newly formulated problems of inculturation and the re-reading of so-called mission history as decolonialized church history.

In the post-conciliar redefinition of plans for theological study in the Catholic Church, however, so far little attention has been paid to mission. We must investigate whether this is a twofold strategy on the part of central organs of administration. Disturbed by secularization and the statistical successes of religious fundamentalism, certain church authorities may in fact be playing with the notion of pushing the 'missionary nature' of the church worldwide in a large-scale fundamentalist offensive. In that case reality would not be experienced as a 'sign of the time' but only as a pastoral irritation.

The first evangelization of Latin America, carried out under the conditions of European expansion, conquest, the colonial system and church patronage, has left behind deep wounds. If these open wounds are not to bleed again as a result of apologetic first-aid dressings, it is important to bring about the healing of the sickness which causes them through the antibodies which are produced in the process of the sickness itself. No one who is weary of reflection, satiated with reality and impenitent will get through the cloud of confusion to new shores. Not only the fruits of the knowledge of good and evil but also the old pomegranate of the 'conquista espiritual' can grow on the tree of re-evangelization.

I. Mission – a burdened concept

Theologians from the once colonialized continents of Africa, Asia and Latin America have avoided the word 'mission' in the period after the Council, and partially replaced it with 'evangelization'. In fact they were able to demonstrate not only that the concept of mission is burdened by its colonial heritage but also that 'mission' in scripture, the church fathers and scholastic theology is not used as a technical term for efforts directed towards the unbaptized. This happened for the first time in the age of European expansion. The connection between political subjection and Christian conversion runs like a scarlet thread through all the so-called first evangelization of Latin America. As one illustration of this, here is the report of the Jesuits of Brazil to the central house of the order, in 1556: 'Experience teaches us that their (the Indios') conversion is very difficult through love; but as these are a servile people, they are ready for anything as a result of fear.'[1]

Behind the paradigm change from 'mission' to 'evangelization' lay the hope that the death of the patient ('mission') would also mean the end of his disease ('mission ideology'). Similar considerations were invoked at the Eighth World Missionary Conference of the World Council of Churches held in Bangkok in 1972/73, in the guise of a 'moratorium on mission'.[2]

To drop the 'mission' paradigm in a zeal to exterminate mission ideology could in itself lead to the formation of a new ideology, the ideology of political innocence, and make Christianity relevant only to itself. To replace the concept of mission by evangelization, in awareness of the way in which 'mission' is burdened by the past, would establish the colonial practice of mission without differentiation and without any alternative, and without offering the slightest guarantee for new conditions. With its approach by means of a patron church Christianity did not primarily compromise the concept of mission, but the gospel and its mediation.

At the same time, the renaming of 'mission' as 'evangelization' in post-conciliar theology also led to reductionist shifts in accent. In practice, up to the end of the 1970s, the Latin American church hardly thought of Africa and Asia, and it paid little heed even to its Indian and Afro-American roots. The hunger for bread and the thirst for righteousness also have cultural presuppositions. Over the long term an African belly cannot be filled with Chinese rice. Slum areas come into being on cultural ruins.

The cultural and historical variety of Latin America could have no more than inadequate illumination under the macro-structural prism of poverty. Moreover the demands of the cultures should not find recognition simply through the back door of the worlds of India and Africa. The identity of the poor must also be differentiated by means of their cultural ecology. Just as Indian peoples have forged the historical insult 'Indio' into a battle slogan, so the emotive term 'mission' which once legitimized colonial praxis can introduce a programme of decolonializing in keeping with the gospel, a programme of historical recollection, pluricultural presence, social solidarity and relevant dialogue.

II. The marginalization of mission studies

In its 1988 document 'Church: Community and Mission', the Brazilian Conference of Bishops called for the incorporation of missiology into the disciplines of the theological curriculum.[3] In this document the bishops begin by stating that the mission *Ad gentes* 'is consolidated and enlarged by the discovery that the whole land is "mission territory"'.[4] The Fourth General Assembly of the Latin American bishops in Santo Domingo in 1992 regretted that there was no programme whatsoever for missionary training in most seminaries for priests (cf. SD 127), and the bishops invited the local churches on the continent 'to integrate specific lectures on mission into the study programme for priests and members of religious orders which will instruct candidates for the priestly office on the importance of the inculturation of the gospel' (SD 128).

Here the Latin American bishops were taking up a proposal made by the Brazilian Conference of Bishops, which in its guidelines for Santo Domingo had indicated that to set the process of inculturation in motion, 'a specific course in mission and cultural anthropology is needed in study seminars'.[5] In the documents mentioned, there was deliberately no longer any sharp distinction between 'mission *Ad gentes*', 'Latin America as a mission area' and 'world mission', because mission theology and the new topic 'inculturation', which was put under missiology, are now quite generally to belong to the basic theological education of priests and laity.

However, inculturation must not be misunderstood in mystical incarnational terms or as a cultural crowbar. Santo Domingo clearly indicates this when it stipulates that the 'open goal of inculturated evangelization must always be the redemption and integral liberation of a particular people or particular group' (SD 243). Thus the current development goes beyond the framework marked out in the mission decree *Ad gentes*, where missiology is still merely conceived of for *ad gentes* missionaries (cf. AG 26).

Two recent papal documents also point in the direction of an integration of missiology into the canon of basic theological formation. For example the encyclical *Redemptoris missio* (1990) states that 'Theological instruction cannot and may not ignore the world mission of the church, the ecumene, the study of the great religions and missiology' (RM 83), and in the most recent document on priestly formation, the post-synodal apostolic writing *Pastores dabo vobis* (1992), John Paul II states that the 'study of missiology and the ecumene, Judaism, Islam and the other non-Christian religions belongs in the field of theology' and is an 'essential ingredient' and an 'instrument' of the new evangelization (PDV 54). Already in *Christifideles laici* and again in *Pastores dabo vobis*, John Paul II defines his ecclesiology in the field of *mysterium*, *communio* and *missio* (cf. CL 8; PDV 12).

This triad of *mysterium*, *communio* and *missio* must be heard in the context of Vatican II. The church as the 'people of God on the way', structured by ministries and charisms, has its origin and its model in the dynamic and the mystery of the trinitarian *communio* and in the *missio* of the Son and the Holy Spirit aimed at the salvation and sanctification of all humankind. In the constitution *Lumen gentium* the Council defined the church from the start as *mysterium* (ch. 1) as distinct from having an understanding of the church centred on the institution. Even before all the differentiation by ministeries and charisms, it stresses the equality and *communio* of all believers which are grounded in baptism (LG, ch. 2). And because this people of God, the church, has a goal, the kingdom of God, it also has a *missio* (LG 15–17). The church has an inner mission, articulated with repentance and conversion, because for it too the kingdom of God is unattainable. But it also has a 'world mission', because at the same time it is an instrument of God for the realization of the kingdom of God. The church is *communio* for the fulfilment of its missionary task (cf. CL 32, SD 55). *Missio* as world mission is that exogamic quest which the church pursues in historical processes of communication and transformation and which preserves it from sheer inwardness or excessive preoccupation with itself.

The missionary zeal which is expressed in quite varied church authorities and the importance of missiology as documented by the magisterium have so far failed to make any mark on the curriculum. Here the question is not of the status of missiology as a theological discipline but rather of the place where the 'missionary nature' of the church is to be communicated theologically. Missiology is largely offered in compact crash courses for missionaries about to set out, and 'inculturation' is dealt with in workshops. In Latin America since 1977, so-called 'Latin American Missionary Congresses' (COMLA) have taken place under the aegis of the 'Papal Missions', which attempt to give new impulses to *Ad gentes* mission. However, missiology should not lead a hand-to-mouth existence in such initiatives, positive though they are in themselves.

In connection with COMLA V, which is to take place in 1995 in Belo Horizonte, Brazil, the Brazilian Conference of Bishops at its plenary in 1993 resolved to institute an 'Ano Missionário'. However, at the same plenary the bishops did not mention missiology at all when amending the programme for philosophical and theological study drawn up in 1984. And in the relevant article of the Roman instructions for the implementation of the Apostolic Constitution *Sapientia Christiana* there is no provision for missiology.[6] An 'ordinary' theological student need never have heard lectures on missiology anywhere in the Catholic Church throughout the world.

But the 'missionary church' which is conjured up so often will not fall into the clergy house like a comet from a documentary heaven. Not only chill reason but also unenlightened zeal can exhaust the mystical glow of *missio*, and a continent Christianized by the colonial system can also export its missionary traumas *Ad gentes*.

III. The silence on inculturation

The curricular marginalization of missiology which in fact gives inculturation no place in the canon of theological disciplines is the first indication of a soft-pedalling of inculturation in the world church. The new Catechism of the Catholic Church (CIC) confirms this. In the

'Thematic Index' of the French, Italian and Colombian editions the word 'inculturation' does not appear at all, although there are relatively frequent references to mission, culture and incarnation. In the key-word index of the German edition, 'Inculturation' is listed four times (CIC 854, 1205, 1206, 1232). However, three of these are false references, because the text itself speaks only of adaptation (CIC 1205f., 1232). Only once does the word 'inculturation' appear, and there in fact with the meaning 'implantation' (CIC 854). The analogy between incarnation and solidarity with the world which was used by the Council (LG 8, GS 32) seems to have been forgotten. So while the Catechism indeed refers to the universal mission of the priest which is associated with ordination, referring to Vatican II (*Presbyterorum ordinis* 10, *Optatam totius* 20), it does not say where and how this mission is to be accomplished (CIC 1565).

Now it could be argued that inculturation is a matter for local churches and does not belong in a world catechism. But this objection must be investigated more closely. First, in this catechism the colonial 'equivalents' of inculturation – integration (nos. 6, 1202), incorporation (nos. 837, 855, 1267, 1396) and assimilation (24, 1205f.) – are used most generously.

Secondly, the apostolic writing *Catechesi tradendae* of 1979 officially introduced the word 'inculturation' into the Catholic Church (CT 53), even if the concept was still left vague. In doing this Pope John Paul II had met the wish of the Fourth General Assembly of the Synod of Bishops (1977), and made it clear that inculturation was indeed to be a semantic imperative in a document on catechesis addressed to the world church. Indeed we must admire the skill with which the final editors of the 'World Catechism' managed to quote the relevant passages of *Catechesi tradendae* (CT 53) without mentioning the decisive word 'inculturation' (cf. CIC 1204). The Brazilian Conference of Bishops also referred to the pluricultural situation of the country in their guidelines for working out diocesan catechisms and called for the inculturation of catechesis into the various 'cultural modes of being'. Inculturation for them means above all 'fear of losing the symbols of the culture in which the catechesis is being given'.[7]

Inculturation as following Jesus in a post-colonial revision of church praxis, the rehabilitation of the other in the church, and solidarity with the poor is not only a catechetical method but also the content of catechesis. Inculturation in itself is always already kerygma about the mystery of the incarnation. As the resolutions of Santo Domingo put it, 'Inculturation is an imperative of the discipleship of Jesus and necessary for the renewal of the disfigured face of the world' (SD 13). The bishops, as the first to be addressed by the new catechism, would certainly have been grateful for an encouraging word that did not see their task as 'teachers of faith and pastors of the church' so much as translation, but rather put it in the field of creative inculturation, inspired by contextual experiences of faith (cf. CIC 9, 11f.).

Also in Santo Domingo it proved that inculturation will still be a lengthy process. It is interesting to note how the Fourth General Assembly of the Latin American bishops passed over without a word the sub-theme of 'Christian culture' which was proposed by Rome and in fact was meant to be a substitute for inculturation. The concept of a 'Christian culture' is an analogous way of speaking of culture, but without using a subject. What is thought of here is not the culture of a people or a social group (GS 53, Puebla 386f.), but a sum of values and so-called Christian points of reference, which can inspire believers in what they do. However, these values, too, must in turn be given a cultural context. Even a metaculture devised in Christian terms must be inculturated if it is to be relevant to social groups. The oligarchies of Latin America have constantly resorted to the concept of 'Christian culture' to maintain the present unjust conditions. The Brazilian bishops already referred to this in their preparatory document for Puebla (1978).[8]

Culture as an environment constructed and dreamed up by social groups, and as a project for life, always relates to the particular world in which these groups live and which constitutes their identity. Therefore evangelization must always start from a reading of these concrete projects and from the spheres of communication offered there. If the church is to show and communicate the love of God (cf. AG 10), it must renounce a universal code and a literal translation of it. It must experience its metalinguistic irrelevance and universal speechlessness in a long process of inculturation and become capable of a new language which is contextual and culture-specific.

It was clear to the Santo Domingo delegates from the start that a 'Christian culture' will not do justice either to the plurality of cultures or to the many ways of being a Christian in Latin America. In defining pastoral priorities, they therefore had to make a significant change to the theme of the conference. The pastoral guidelines to be decided on were indeed to have some relation to the theme of 'new evangelization, furthering of humanity, Christian culture'. So the bishops defined their priorities as 'new evangelization' and 'furthering of humanity' but not as 'Christian culture' with priorities on an 'inculturated evangelization'. In so doing they returned from the abstract macrostructure of a 'Christian

culture' to the sphere of social groups and peoples, to the sphere of the poor
and the other.

At present three quite different sectors can be made out in this confusion
over inculturation. Some people simply attempt to avoid the word
inculturation as far as possible. Others regard it as 'unavoidable' and
attempt to fill out inculturation with preconciliar paradigms, i.e. with
'conversion', 'church founding', 'integration' and 'assimilation'. Even the
Final Document of Santo Domingo has not yet freed itself from colonialist
and macho language. The document states that Christian culture and faith
must 'penetrate' (SD 35, 161, 229, 302f.) and 'invade' (SD 229) the
cultures and hearts of the peoples to correct their errors. A third group
speaks of inculturation as readiness to get rid of ethnocentrism and
colonialism, and talks of readiness for dialogue and the recognition of the
other as a principle of identity for the church.

IV. The burden of reality

Parallel to the soft-pedalling of inculturation, on the mission scene there
are also signs of a fundamental controversy over the status of reality for
missionary praxis and reflection. In Santo Domingo it became very clear
how much importance certain sectors attach to no longer writing church
documents along the lines of 'see reality – make a theological judgment –act
pastorally'; in each case a contextless theology is presented to a reality
filtered through 'pastoral demands'. Thus the 'new methods' of re-
evangelization, to which reference is so often made (SD 1, 29, 101), often
turn out to be rusty old weapons.

The fear of coming into contact with reality casts long shadows over the
hermeneutics of history. On the occasion of the discussion of the 500 years
of conquest and evangelization, wide circles of the church were ready to
concede abuses on the part of 'individual baptized', but not a structural
blindness of the church. In fact the preaching of violence in Christianity
did not come from unfaithful outsiders but from church fathers and saints
legitimated by the institution. One need only read the sermons on the Jews
by Augustine and Ambrose, or Bernard of Clairvaux's crusade preaching.
So the potential of the churches for peace cannot legitimately be played off
against the potential for violence of individual laity, members of orders or
national states; there is need to reflect on the potential of Christianity as a
whole for violence.[9]

After the subjection of the Aztec empire Cortes called on the
Franciscans to give a new ideological orientation to the defeated. In a so-

called 'dialogue of faith', the Franciscans taught the Aztec leaders and priests that they had found 'nothing right, nothing true, nothing worth believing' in their religious traditions, 'only empty words.'[10]

How different such a religious dialogue could have been had been shown 250 years earlier by Ramon Lull in his *Book of the Heathen and the Three Wise Men*.[11] As though he had foreseen the scenario of 1492 with the subjection of the Moors, the expulsion of the Jews and the conquest of the Indios, Lull constructs a dialogue on the faith between a heathen and three wise men who represent the three monotheistic world religions of Islam, Judaism and Christianity. After each of the three wise men had had the opportunity to present his religion, the heathen burst out into joyful praise of God. Quite free of any proselytizing zeal, the wise men refrained from asking to which religion the heathen had converted. Given the division between them, the 'conversion of the heathen' was not their priority. Before they parted, they asked one another for forgiveness and resolved to continue the religious dialogue for the sake of the peace of humankind.

Violence in the process of evangelization does not pay. Bernardino de Sahagún, who reconstructed the so-called 'dialogue of faith' between Indios and Franciscans forty years later, acknowledged that the destruction of Indian religion among the descendants of the Aztec empire had brought with it a moral decline which the missionaries could not halt.[12] And the recognition of slavery as a 'regular' method of evangelization because it meant the saving of souls did not make any 'classical' Christians out of the Afro-Americans.[13] As almost all the religious orders of colonial Latin America were slave-owners, the 'unknown holocaust' of Afro-Americans cannot legitimately be foisted on 'government officials and private individuals' or 'baptized who did not live out their faith' (cf. SD 30). Ecclesiastical historical apologetic which traumatizes the past through forgetfulness can be a new form of structural violence.

V. A refusal to repent

The apologetic historical account in the Santo Domingo document (SD 16–21), prepared by a symposium in Rome held by the Papal Commission for Latin America (CAL),[14] is closely connected with an inability to put a comprehensive request for forgiveness to Indios and Afro-Americans. The demand put to other peoples in missionary praxis to forget their culture and history always also corrupts the church's own memory. But promises of solidarity in the present are credible only when they also take responsibility for the past.

In their 'Guidelines for Santo Domingo' the Brazilian bishops asked the Indian peoples and the Afro-Americans for forgiveness over their 'failure and participation' in the Conquista.[15] The church, they said, has not recognized the presence of God in their cultures and has tolerated or even participated in their destruction; it has justified the slavery of the negroes with the gospel and derived material benefit from this slavery. The Indian peoples and negroes of Latin America have always lived on the periphery of the institutional church and society. Finally, the Brazilian bishops promised to regard their unconditional solidarity as an integral part of the new evangelization.

On 17 October 1992, in the name of thirty-three bishops, Bishop Benedito Ulho proposed to the plenary assembly of Santo Domingo that they should prepare a ceremony of repentance for the quincentenary of the evangelization of the Americas. Two days later, the Argentinian archbishop Italo di Stefano spoke out against such a ceremony. He spoke of three myths about the Indios. First there had been no genocide of the Indios. Secondly, the Indian past had not been a paradise. Thirdly, there had not been five hundred years of resistance against Christianity because the Indios knew that they were better off with Christianity than with their old religions. According to di Stefano, a request for forgiveness would be used by 'ideological sectors' against the church and would betray a guilt complex which would weaken missionary zeal.[16]

In the toing and froing over the request for forgiveness, on 21 October the pope finally intervened in the discussion from Rome. During his general audience he gave a brief address on the petition for forgiveness in the Lord's Prayer (Matt 6.12). 'The prayer of the Redeemer is addressed to the Father and at the same time to those people to whom many injustices have been done. We pray to these people incessantly for forgiveness. This prayer of forgiveness is directed above all to the first inhabitants of the new earth, to the Indios and also to those who were deported as slaves from Africa to perform hard labour. Forgive us our trespasses . . . . : this prayer too is part of evangelization . . . '[17] Despite the 'golden bridge' of the papacy, Santo Domingo limited itself to a petition for forgiveness, addressed only to God, 'for unfaithfulness to his good gifts' (SD 1). The only place at which the document speaks of 'errors' is in referring to the errors of the cultures not yet touched by the gospel (SD 230). The document speaks of penitence only in connection with the sacrament of penance (SD 46, 80, 151). Here a symbolic indication of readiness to repent would have given radical credibility to the preaching of the kingdom of God for the Indios and Afro-Americans.

VI. Beyond confusion

The *missio* of the church could easily disappear from view in the mist produced by the historical loading of the concept of mission, the officially documented importance of mission and missiology and the blocking of its introduction into the curriculum, the confusion over the soft-pedalling of inculturation, a weariness with reality and an unreadiness to repent. But the identification of the grey blocks of stone in the mist can be the first step towards avoiding accidents, even if 'the dawn of a Christian spring' (RM 86) cannot yet be made out in this confused mission scenario.

The confused mission scenario is the reflection of a confused world scenario in which the 'great stories', the stories of the victors, have lost their credibility. In the perspective of the victorious neo-liberal market which has no subjects, all over the world an increasing number of people are ceasing to be the economic or legal subjects of a state. Neither justice nor alms are to be expected from the 'invisible hand' of neo-liberal market structures. No responsible subject can be made out behind the 'great story'. Projects for life, whether based on culture or the gospel, are in particular danger. For an increasing number of those who are excluded, who do not participate in the markets of opinion, work or consumer goods, there are no 'great hopes'.

In this scenario, what is the meaning of *missio*, as a historical quest which brings hope? How is mission to be taken forward without Catholic kings and a patron church, without a peasantry indebted to the Ancien Régime, without Romanized Christianity and without a 'Christian' workforce?

Mission, including *Ad gentes* mission, is increasingly taking the side of the excluded majority in the world, those without language, land, shelter and work, who live outside the statistics and systems of work and market. The excluded and their actual resistance to the subjectless 'structures of death' indicate that microstructural hopes could lie behind any 'great story'. A gospel inculturated in the worlds in which the excluded live strengthens the power of the 'little story' to resist. Inculturated evangelization can be the communication of a hope which stems from a 'little story'. Inculturation can reveal once again the non-systemic character and anti-systemic imperative of the gospel.

The Catholic Church in Brazil will dedicate its fast, 'Brotherliness and the Excluded', to these people who are excluded. The scriptural word chosen for it comes from the judgment speech in Matthew, 'Lord, was it you?' So the issue is the judgment of God in the face of the hungry and the alien, the sick and the prisoner, those excluded from the security and the provisions offered by the state and the market. They live and hope in this world without being of this world. They represent the *necessary* hope which is no longer statistically relevant in the projections of the future.

Thus the church and theology face a changed reality and new demands. The prime concern is no longer the 'exodus' from a slave-owning society; nor is it only a matter of those exploited by the 'system', the workers or the lowest paid. With those excluded from the 'system' the missionary church has a new majority in the world. Those who are excluded are no 'working class' represented by the trade unions. Their grief brings awareness but no articulated *communio*. That can be the new task of *missio* (cf. CL 32). Here we shall have to think of the definition of missionary priorities. In the face of the winter mist of the great church, and political and economic hopelessness, they represent the real horizon of hope for the world. They are God's project for the future 'in earthen vessels' (II Cor. 4.6f).

Translated by John Bowden

Notes

1. 'Por amor hé mi dificultosa a sua conversão, mas, como hé gente servil, por medo faxem tudo', in S. Leite (ed.), *Cartas dos primeiros jesuítas do Brasil*, 2, São Paulo 1952, 271.
2. The discussion of the moratorium was in Section 2, 'Churches Renewed in Mission'.
3. Cf. Conferência Nacional dos Bispos do Brasil (CNBB), *Igreja: Comunhão e missão na evangelização dos povos, no mundo do trabalho, da política e da cultura*, Documentos da CNBB 40, São Paulo 1988, no. 124.
4. Ibid., no. 39.
5. CNBB, *Das diretrizes para Santo Domingo*, Documentos da CNBB 48, São Paulo 1992, no. 42a.
6. Cf. *Formação dos presbiteros na Igreja do Brasil. Diretrizes básicas*, Documentos da CNBB 30, São Paulo 1984; *Orientações para os estudos filosóficos e teológicos*, Estudos da CNBB 51, São Paulo 1987; *Disposições da Sagrada congregação para a Educação Católica para a exacta aplicação da Constitutição Apostólica Sapientia Chritiana*, Art. 51, Rome 1979.
7. *Textos e manuais de catequese*, Estudos da CNBB 53, São Paulo 1987, nos. 56–62: 6of.
8. Cf. CNBB, *Subsidios para Puebla*, Documentos da CNBB 13, São Paulo 1978, no. 53.
9. Cf. P. Suess, 'Bekehrungsauftrag und Conquista', in M. Sievernich et al. (ed.), *Conquista und Evangelisation. Fünfhundert Jahre Orden in Lateinamerica*, Mainz 1992, 201–22.

10. M. Leon-Portilla (ed.), *Los Diálogos de 1524 segun el texto de fray Bernardino de Sahagún y sus colaboradores indigenas*, Mexico 1986, 113, 155, 193f.

11. *El libro dèl gentil e dels tres savis*, in R. Lull, *Obres essencials* 1, Barcelona 1957, 107–272.

12. Cf. B. de Sahagún, *Historia general de las cosas de la Nueva Espana* (4 vols), Mexico 1981, here Vol. 3, book 10, ch. 27, 159f.

13. Cf. P. Suess, 'Zur Geschichte und Ideologie von Sklaverei und Sklavenbefreiung in Brasilien', *Münchener Theologische Zeitschrift* 43/3, 1992, 293–313. Similarly REB 51/204 (December 1991), 902–21.

14. Cf. Pontificia Commissio pro America, *Historia da evangelização da America. Simposio Internacional. Actas: 11–14. 5. 1992*, Vatican City 1992.

15. CNBB, *Das diretrizes* (n. 5), 18f.

16. Cf. Boletin de Prensa 16, 20 October 1992, Anexo 1.

17. Boletin de Prensa 22, 23 October 1992, Anexo, 12.

Inculturation: How to Proceed in a Pastoral Context

Thomas Groome

The pastoral task

How can a pastoral minister be intentional about the task of inculturation? Is there a recommended pastoral approach that consistently honours its intent? My article addresses this question of existential praxis. It claims that unless the pastoral minister has the necessary convictions and an effective approach, the 'habit', shall we say, to mediate between gospel and culture in a way that moves beyond translation and accommodation to inculturation, commitment to inculturation is only rhetorical.

There is never a cultureless Christianity and never yet a fully Christian culture. Thus, all pastoral ministers are to be agents of inculturation, to mediate between some 'gospel' and some 'culture'. But clearly this pastoral task is intensified for ministers in cultures that are new or recent to Christian faith, in contexts that have been touched little already by any of the various cultures of Christianity; this is the situation that I have particularly in mind. Regardless of the intensity of the task, however, all pastoral agents need the requisite convictions and an intentional approach to inculturation.

Though it has been amply described and defined in previous articles, I should explain briefly how I understand 'inculturation' as a pastoral task; this is a necessary prelude to my proposal for a pastoral approach to realizing it. My starting premise is that inculturation of Christian faith has the primary purpose of advancing the coming of God's reign in a particular time and place.

The 'reign of God' is a comprehensive symbol of God's intentions for all creation. In the Hebrew tradition, these intentions are epitomized in Gods vision of *shalom* – of peace and justice, love and freedom, wholeness and fullness of life for all humankind, and the integrity of God's creation. In Christian faith, Jesus understood the purpose of his life and work as the realization of God's reign. For Jesus, the reign of God is accomplished as the hungry are fed, the impoverished are cared for, the sick are healed, the sinners are reconciled, the marginalized are included, the outcasts are welcomed, the oppressed set free, the poor hear the Good News of God's love, and all are brought toward fullness of life (see Luke 4. 16–21; Matt. 11. 4–6; Matt. 25. 31–46; John 10. 10, etc.). And the greatest commandment of the reign of God in Jesus subsumes the mandate of justice into the totalizing and radical law of love; totalizing in that we are to love God with all our mind, heart, soul and strength, and our neighbour as ourself (see Luke 10. 27, etc.), and radical in that for Jesus, 'neighbour' knows no limits and measures our love for God. As with the praxis of Jesus, the reign of God always symbolizes the pastoral purpose of his disciples, and should guide and evaluate their approach to inculturation.

Always with the undergirding purpose of God's reign in Jesus, Christian inculturation is a *dialectical encounter* between an already cultured version of Christian faith and another culture that is either new to Christianity or has aspects not yet explicitly permeated by it. As an 'encounter' it is a *two-way* exchange – from 'gospel' to culture and from culture to 'gospel' – and as 'dialectical' it reflects a *threefold* dynamic of affirming and cherishing, of refusing or questioning, and of moving on to new and transformed possibilities for both 'gospel' and culture.

Taking the dialectic first from the 'gospel' side of the encounter: there will be aspects of a particular culture that Christian faith will affirm and cherish as life-giving and of God's reign; there will be cultural aspects that Christianity may reject or question as problematic to God's reign; and Christian faith will invite that culture to greater transformation toward the reign of God. Likewise, from the culture's side of the encounter: there will be aspects of this culturally laden 'gospel' that it will affirm and recognize as life-giving and of God's reign; there will be aspects that this culture of encounter will question or find problematic in its context; and this culture will 'go beyond' what it encounters as it appropriates this instance of Christianity to itself to forge an indigenous and enriched expression of Christian faith.

In this dialectic, the enrichment of the culture fostered by Christianity is not a negation of it, though its problematics for God's reign are critiqued and challenged by 'the gospel'. Rather, an encounter of inculturation affirms what is true and life-giving in the context, and builds upon these signs of God's reign already present to offer new possibilities of personal and social transformation. Likewise, the encounter with a 'different' culture offers Christian faith the gift of a unique expression of itself that enriches the whole body of Christ. It helps the universal Christian community to appropriate aspects of 'the gospel' not realized this way before, and helps to unfold the 'surplus of meaning' and value that ever remains in this 'storehouse' of God's reign (see Matt. 13. 52).

Drawing these reflections together, I describe inculturation more precisely as *a dialectical encounter between Christian faith and a particular culture in which the culture is affirmed, challenged, and transformed toward God's reign, and in which Christian faith is likewise affirmed, challenged, and enriched by this unique instance of its realization*. We can now return to our central question of how to proceed with inculturation in a pastoral context.

Requisite convictions for inculturation

Being effective agents of inculturation depends less on people's overt method than on the operative convictions they bring to their ministry. Inculturation is always more a question of *phronesis* than of *techne*, of practical wisdom than of a particular technique. And as Aristotle would have it, practical wisdom must be informed by sound principles that one cherishes as one's own convictions and can implement in particular circumstances.[1] To be a pastoral agent of inculturation suggests at least four foundational convictions that the minister should 'own' and bring to every instance of the gospel/culture encounter.

1. *There is never a cultureless Christianity nor a faithless culture*. In practice, the first of these companion convictions should prevent pastoral agents from totalizing any one expression of Christian faith, and the second reminds them that God's saving presence and self-disclosure is always 'already there' in every culture, long before explicitly Christian faith arrives. Together they encourage the genuine encounter and conversation of inculturation.

Much of the pastoral praxis of the church has not recognized that every expression of Christianity is culturally laden, including that of the first Christian communities. Until recently we often assumed that the creed, code and cult of Christian faith were transcendental-like, above and beyond 'the effects' of human history. Christian texts, symbols and sources were considered absolved from historical and social conditionedness; they were presumed to reflect 'knowledge' that is universal, objective and neutral. But contemporary awareness that all tradition carries within it 'the effects of its history' (Gadamer), that all knowledge and identity is socially conditioned, means that the symbols of Christian faith reflect the culture of particular time and place. Far from relativizing Christian faith, awareness of its historicity prevents it from becoming a hardened ideology and enables it to continue as a 'living' tradition (see 2. below). Putting our culture-laden understanding of Christianity 'at risk' by encountering an 'other' perspective or context, is precisely what gives the tradition new life.

Regarding the faith 'already there' in every culture, again Christians must admit to previous patterns of blindness. Christian missionaries to non-Christian contexts have often viewed the indigenous people and their culture as essentially 'pagan', their religious beliefs and practices as spurious, and have presumed that they were bringing God's word and presence to these faithless people. A favourite image for their prior state was 'darkness'; and the missionaries brought them 'light', especially the 'light of Christ'.

By contrast, agents of inculturation should be convinced that God has always been 'here' in this context, and with saving presence and self-disclosure, since the dawn of history. Christian missionaries do not 'bring God' to anyone, since God is always already present ahead of them. To say otherwise would deny two central aspects of Catholic Christian faith, namely the universality of God's love and the principle of sacramentality. To maintain that the culture of encounter is simply 'pagan' and faithless would imply that God is present among and has led only Christians aright, and is absent from and has led all others astray; surely a cynical and sectarian God rather than one who loves all humankind. The Christian and especially Catholic principle of sacramentality reflects the conviction that God mediates Godself to humankind through the ordinary events and things of everyday existence. As Rahner wrote, 'the very commonness of everyday things harbours the eternal marvel and silent mystery of God and (God's) grace'.[2] But this is true of everyone's 'everyday' and not simply of Christians.

This sentiment was well expressed as 'the mind of the church' by Vatican II's *Declaration on Non-Christian Religions* (*Nostra Aetate*). The *Declaration* begins with the foundational principle that 'God's providence, manifestations of goodness, and saving designs extend to all people'.[3] In consequence, 'the Catholic Church rejects nothing that is true and holy' in other religious traditions and, the Council makes explicit, non-Christian traditions 'often reflect a ray of that Truth which enlightens all people'.[4]

This does not diminish the preeminence and normativity of Jesus Christ for Christian faith. As the Declaration insists, the church 'proclaims and must ever proclaim Christ, "the way, the truth, and the life"'.[5] And yet, affirming Jesus as the apex of God's self-disclosure and saving action in human history does not preclude openness to and appreciation for God's revelation in traditions and cultures that are 'other'. In fact, Christians should enter into 'dialogue and cooperation with the followers of other religions, and in witness of Christian faith and life, acknowledge, preserve, and promote the spiritual and moral goods found among these people, as well as the values in their society and culture'.[6]

How relevant these sentiments of the Council are to the pastoral task of inculturation! They encourage the genuine encounter between 'gospel' and culture that is inculturation. They require that pastoral agents recognize the cultural conditionedness of all expressions of Christian faith, and that they constantly be alert to uncover and encourage in this context what should be affirmed and raised up as of God's reign. These 'signs' may be built upon and refurbished by the Christian 'gospel', but must never be nullified or diminished.

2. *The 'story' and 'vision' of Christian faith continues to unfold throughout history.* In practice, Christian faith continues as a living tradition by being realized as a 'current event' in new times and places. Its vitality cannot be served by mere repetition or direct application, but demands indigenization in every cultural context.

If pastoral agents perceive Christian revelation as a static and closed expression of the fullness of divine truth, they will oppose genuine dialogue or encounter with their cultural context. Clearly, true inculturation demands the conviction that the 'story' of Christian faith, (i.e. all the symbols that express and carry its truth and ethic over time),[7] is still unfolding, that it has depths yet to be fathomed, and a 'surplus of meaning' (Ricoeur) that will never be exhausted. Likewise the 'vision' of this tradition (i.e. our present living of it toward the reign of God) is always evolving and in need of reform, and ever calls us into greater faithfulness until the completion of God's reign. Agents of inculturation need to be convinced of this 'unfolding' sense of Christian faith, as the faith of a pilgrim people.

The Israelites were convinced that God could always 'do something new' (Isa. 43, 19). The Hebrew scriptures often retell or reconstruct older texts and traditions as appropriate to a new context; Exodus is remembered and interpreted differently during the monarchy from during the exile. Jesus echoed this sentiment when he declared that 'Every scribe who is learned in the reign of God is like the head of a household who can bring from (the) storeroom both the new and the old' (Matt. 13. 52). At the end of his life, he intimated that there was 'much more' that would unfold after him with the help of 'the Spirit of truth' who would 'guide to all truth' (see John 16. 12–13). An eminent first instance of this unfolding of revelation took place at the Council of Jerusalem. The apostolic Christian community had to face an 'other' perspective from an 'other' culture, a Gentile refusal of Mosaic dietary laws, and of circumcision for male converts. After communal discernment, they reached a decision that 'seemed good to the Holy Spirit and to us' (Acts 15. 28), to dispense with circumcision; this was a significant 'new moment' for the whole Christian community.

This openness to development in response to new situations and cultures continued throughout Christian history. It is epitomized in the particularly Catholic claim that the ongoing 'tradition' of the faith community is a necessary companion to scripture as source of God's revelation. As *Dei Verbum* states, 'Sacred tradition and sacred Scripture form one sacred deposit of the word of God.'[8] And again, 'both sacred tradition and sacred Scripture are to be accepted and venerated', because 'it is not from scripture alone' that the church draws 'what has been revealed'.[9] But contrary to a conservative posture that tradition is an argument against 'development', our very respect for it reflects the conviction that our understanding and living of 'the faith handed on' has unfolded since biblical times and continues to unfold. This, too, was 'the mind' of Vatican II.

Dei Verbum began by reiterating: 'The Christian dispensation . . . as the new and definitive covenant, will never pass away, and we now await no further new public revelation.'[10] In this sense, Christian revelation was complete, at least in its primordial form, with the death of the last apostle. However, our appropriation and understanding of this revelation remains an ongoing project that continues throughout history. The Council states: 'the tradition which comes from the apostles *develops* in the Church with the help of the Holy Spirit. For there is a *growth in the understanding* of the realities and the words which have been handed down.' Then the Council declared, 'as the centuries succeed one another, the Church constantly *moves forward toward the fullness of divine truth* until the words of God reach their complete fulfillment in her'[11] (emphases added). This was a rather amazing admission for a community that had consistently claimed already to possess the 'fullness of truth'.

The sentiment of the Council that 'the tradition . . . develops' finds warrant in contemporary literature on hermeneutics. Let me note first that this should not surprise because the dynamic of inculturation is essentially hermeneutical. As Ricoeur writes, 'To "make one's own" what was previously "foreign" remains the ultimate aim of all hermeneutics.'[12] The central point of relevance here is that every authentic interpretation of a 'text' of a tradition in a new situation is, in fact, a new moment of understanding, and a new form of the tradition. (Contemporary hermeneutics takes 'text' to mean any symbol of meaning or tradition.)

David Tracy has developed the helpful image of a 'classic' for the perduring 'texts' of tradition.[13] As such, 'classics' are marked by both 'permanence and excess of meaning'. The perduring nature of 'classics' is that they always mean 'something of genuine interest here and now, in this time and place';[14] they can always address themselves to new situations. Their 'excess of meaning' signifies that they can always 'mean' more than they 'meant'. In Ricoeur's phrase, they have a 'surplus of meaning', or there is always a 'horizon of meaning' in front of them. And this 'surplus' is uncovered through 'ever-changing receptions' in new times and places.[15] Given the classics' permanence and excess of meaning they 'demand interpretation, never mere repetition'.[16]

Gadamer likens interpretation to a 'conversation'.[17] In the 'to and fro' encounter between interpreter and 'text', both sides must be honoured. To understand in *this* situation, interpreters must bring the 'effects' of their own history (i.e. their cultural heritage) into conversation with the 'effective history' reflected in the 'text'. The intent is to discern not simply what the 'text' meant but what it means, its significance for this situation. As such, and as Gadamer emphasizes, hermeneutics always has the interest of 'application'.[18] This does not mean simply applying a fixed past meaning to a novel situation, but rather that the tradition gives and gains new life as its significance is realized in a new situation. For Gadamer, 'each new effort to understand reflects . . . a new form of the tradition itself'.[19]

In other words, authentic understanding of a classic is always a *situated* event of traditioning: 'the text . . . if it is to be understood properly – i.e., according to the claim it makes – must be understood at every moment, in every concrete situation, in a new and different way. Understanding here is always application.'[20] Such understanding amounts to a 'fusion of horizons', and this 'fusion' is a new and broader horizon for both 'text' and present interpreter. By honouring rather than collapsing the 'tension between the text and the present', each leads the other into the horizon of meaning 'in front of' them.[21]

Apropos our concern for inculturation, these insights from hermeneutics mean that a genuine encounter between 'gospel' and culture must hold new possibilities for both. And this requires that pastoral agents be convinced and committed to the ongoingness of Christian story and vision, and open to the potential of every 'other' culture to bring new life to Christian faith through its inculturation.

3. *Each cultural expression of Christian faith should be profoundly unique, while remaining bonded in essential unity with all other expressions.* Practically, this requires pastoral agents to seek out and encourage what makes for an indigenous and unique expression of Christian faith in this culture, and at the same time to help maintain its bond with the universal body of Christ.

All instances of Catholic Christianity should have a profound bond of solidarity in faith, hope and love, and their unity in faith should coalesce around truths that are essential to Catholic identity. By 'essential' I mean the beliefs and values that are constitutive of Catholicism, that make it what it is. As Vatican II asserted, 'there exists an order or "hierarchy" of truths, since they vary in their relationship to the foundation of the Christian faith.'[22] 'Essential' or constitutive truths are clearly those on the upper echelons of this hierarchy.

Unity in faith is possible around the 'essentials' because the very core of Catholic Christianity is constituted by truths and values that can find resonance in all human hearts – albeit appropriated differently, that can have particular meaning in every culture and are limited to none. As such, the core convictions of Christian faith, though always expressed and indigenized through particular cultural symbols, can be transhistorical and transcultural. For example, the 'paschal mystery' is the perennial experience of humankind; what human being does not encounter the possibility of death and yet cling to the hope of new life every day? The symbol of hypostatic union of divinity and humanity in Jesus, though intuited and expressed in a myriad of different ways, can be presented to appeal to something deeply human in all people as they claim their authentic humanity and yet recognize their inmost desires and potentialities. Likewise, though wondrously diverse in content and protocol, the symbol of a shared meal has deep meaning in every culture, and lends itself to a sacramental perspective that bonds participants together and with the divine. And the Catholic moral tradition of a 'natural law' reflects the conviction that, though always historically mediated and accommodated, all people have 'by design' the ability to know the intentions of 'the

Designer'. In sum, the church's very claim to 'catholicity' reflects the conviction that the truths and values of Christianity can be appropriated by diverse cultures, and according to the mode of the receiver, while maintaining a profound unity in the universal community of faith.

This unity is better realized through diversity than uniformity; it is most authentic when each cultural expression of Christian faith is unique to itself. Every instance should have its own soul and quality that moulds its discrete identity as an expression of Christian faith. There is an ancient scholastic conviction that all revelation must be appropriated and expressed according to the mode of its receivers. And for every people, that 'mode' entails the symbols of their particular culture. Thus, to appropriate and respond to Christian faith in a way integral to their identity, every people must do so through symbols and patterns indigenous to their culture. This will be a unique expression of Christian faith.

The theological warrant for distinct cultural expressions of Christian faith is the very incarnational principle that stands at the heart of Christianity. In faith we believe that 'in the fullness of time' (Heb. 1. 2) God's own Word 'was made flesh and dwelt among us' (John 1. 14) in Jesus of Nazareth. Jesus' identity was shaped by his cultural context as a first-century Palestinian Jew. Likewise, the first expressions of his gospel reflected the language, mores, and ethos of that culture. Now the 'word' that is Christian faith must be 'made flesh' over and over again in the life of every Christian and in the culture of every time and place. As with its first incarnation, every incarnation thereafter, to be authentic, must find expression in the culture of its time and place.

Inculturation, then, requires pastoral agents to encourage people to appropriate and express Christian faith through the symbols of their own culture. Likewise they must serve as vigilant 'defends of the bond' of this people with the whole body of Christ. Both aspects are their 'Catholic' responsibility.

4. *The values of God's reign should be reflected in the very process of inculturation.* In practice this means that the approach and style used by pastoral agents should be marked by the values of God's reign, and especially by radical love.

I noted earlier that God's reign symbolizes the purpose of inculturation. As with all Christian ministry, its intent is to promote peace and justice, love and freedom, wholeness and fullness of life for all people and the integrity of God's creation. This is the transforming purpose of Christian inculturation for both individual lives and its cultural contexts.

My point with this fourth conviction, however, is to turn this purpose back upon the process and practice of inculturation itself. The very approaches that pastoral agents take to inculturation should reflect the values of God's reign. For example, they are to act with justice by respecting the culture and promoting the rights and dignity of all; to disparage or demean is injustice. They are to proceed peaceably by encouraging people to come to their own word and cultural expression of Christian faith; to impose a 'foreign' system is violence. Their approach should be consciousness-raising and empower people to become intentional and creative historical agents; a 'banking approach' (Freire) will colonize and encourage dependency.

Above all, the process of inculturation should be marked by the ultimate Christian law of love, and by radical love in that 'neighbour' knows neither exception nor favouritism. Without such love, pastoral agents can promote the terror of bigoted sectarianism. Such sectarianism sees the 'other' as an enemy that deserves to be destroyed, if not domesticated to become 'like us'. It insists hegemonically that 'our particular' must reign as *the* universal'. Its intent is 'the empire' rather than the reign of God.

The evidence of history should prevent any naiveté about the capacity of Christian evangelists to promote bigoted sectarianism. We have often preached 'the gospel' in ways that insisted upon one cultural expression of Christianity, and implicitly, at least, encouraged hatred for anything or anyone 'other'. As the church enters what Karl Rahner has called its 'third moment' – its move out of European cultural confinement to become a genuine 'world' church, (and as the 'old world' undergoes what Pope John Paul II calls a 'new evangelization'), let us not make the same mistake again. Christian inculturation must encourage the particular as an instance of the universal, promote diversity as the only fitting human mode of unity. This requires radical love as the *modus operandi* of inculturation; it will not be achieved with less.

A pastoral approach to inculturation

In the light of the above description of inculturation and its requisite convictions, a recommended approach to its pastoral praxis might be described as 'conversation'.

I have already noted that many theorists of hermeneutics favour this term as a description of what should take place between a reader and a text.[23] Gadamer describes conversation as 'a process of coming to understanding. Thus it belongs to every true conversation that each person opens himself to the other, truly accepts his point of view as valid and transposes himself into the other to such an extent that he understands not the particular individual but what he says.'[24] However, Tracy's description seems to emphasize the dialectical nature of conversation more than Gadamer, and for this reason I prefer it for the process of inculturation. Tracy writes, 'Conversation is a game with some hard rules: say only what you mean; listen to and respect what the other says, however different or other; be willing to correct or defend your opinions if challenged by the conversation partner; be willing to argue if necessary, to confront if demanded, to endure necessary conflict, to change your mind if the evidence suggests it.'[25]

The 'conversation' of inculturation requires honesty and integrity of the partners, respect for each other, and a willingness to enter into the kind of listening that 'crosses over' through empathy. Its participants should have the good will to seek the truth rather than to gain strategic advantage. It requires a willingness to reflect critically on how one's own context and interests have shaped one's views, and openness to uncover previously distorted or repressed communication. Such an ideal, of course, is never fully realized but, as with Habermas' 'ideal type' of 'communicative competence',[26] creating conversations that at least approximate this ideal is the task of pastoral agents of inculturation.

The substance of the conversation of inculturation is about this culture and the 'life' that goes on here, about the story and vision of Christian faith, and about appropriating these two to each other – this 'life world' and this faith tradition – in ways transforming for both. These three foci of the conversation suggest a particular dynamic and process that can be employed to facilitate it. I have written in detail about such a conversational process elsewhere[27] and call it a 'shared Christian praxis approach'. My development of it has pertained particularly to religious education. Here I propose it as a fitting approach to the task of inculturation.[28]

Shared Christian praxis has five prototypical 'movements'. Though the movements have a logic to them, they are more dynamics to permeate the conversation than a lock-step process. In a pastoral situation or encounter the movements would rarely unfold in their logical sequence but would alternate, be repeated, combine, have prominence and recede, in a variety of configurations. I will review them briefly here as five activities (verbs) that permeate an intentional process of inculturation.

Movement 1. *Expressing*: The conversation of inculturation constantly brings participants to express their own life-world, to signify how they perceive what is going on within them, in their life, in their culture and context. Such 'naming' (Freire) of their 'praxis' in the world can be done in myriad ways, but the pastoral agent's task is to invite and encourage participants to 'speak their own word' about their life-world, and then to model the quality of listening and probing required of true conversation.

Movement 2. *Critical Reflecting*: Critical reflection is the process of uncovering the genesis and import of one's culture and context. Such reflection enhances both personal conversion and ecclesial and social transformation. Pastoral agents can encourage participants to reflect critically (themselves included) by posing questions that engage reason, memory and imagination apropos their historical situation: reason to discern the reasons behind present praxis, the interests being served, its undergirding assumptions and ideologies, and so on; memory to re-member the personal and social history of their life-world; imagination to envision likely and preferred outcomes, what can and should be done, new possibilities, and so on. Essentially, critical reflection as a dynamic of the conversation of inculturation means inviting people to reflect on their life in this context, to remember its history, and to imagine its future with a sense of agency for it.

Movement 3. *Giving Direct Access to Christian Story and Vision*: Pastoral agents of inculturation are always responsible for seeing to it that the people in this context have direct access to the story and vision of Christian faith. I say 'direct' access because the more people can personally encounter the symbols of Christian faith (scripture, tradition, liturgy, etc.), the more likely they are to bring their own cultural 'story and vision' into conversation with Christian story and vision. (To illustrate, the catechism approach used in much past evangelization did not lend such 'direct' access.) I use the term 'access'[29] because, instead of imposing upon or mediating to, it signals putting people themselves in immediate conversation with the symbols of Christian faith. As they have such access, the pastoral agent is constantly to encourage participants in a dialectical appropriation of Christian faith to their own culture. This is the dynamic intent of movement 4!

Movement 4. *Appropriating*: This movement highlights the dialectical dynamic that should permeate the whole pastoral praxis of inculturation. As noted, the exchange is between this peoples' culture and life-world, and the culturally laden version of Christian faith that is brought into their context. Here the conversation should have the full force of the dialectical encounter I outlined under 'Pastoral Task' above. As people discern what is to be affirmed, questioned, and moved beyond in their culture and in the version of 'gospel' brought to them, they can appropriate Christian faith according to their own cultural mode of receiving it, and will express it in symbols both indigenous to their culture and appropriate to Christian faith.

Movement 5. *Living and Transforming Faith*: The call to Christian faith is always an invitation to *metanoia*, to personal conversion in Christian discipleship after the 'way' of Jesus, and to participate in the upbuilding of God's reign in one's historical context. The conversation of inculturation should include this call to discipleship; it is to invite people to decision about how to live their Christian faith, and contribute to renewing the church and transforming their social/cultural context toward God's reign. This call to discipleship should indeed be one of invitation rather than expectation, and pastoral agents must encourage participants to express their response in indigenous ways.

I propose this 'shared Christian praxis approach' as one suggestive pattern for sponsoring the dynamics of inculturation; I'm sure there are other ways. However, it would seem that the encounter of inculturation demands some such intentional approach to the pastoral 'conversation'.

Notes

1. See, for example, *Nicomachean Ethics*, Bk. 6, Ch. 11. 7.
2. Karl Rahner, *Belief Today*, New York 1967, 4. Here Rahner is echoing the sentiment of his Jesuit founder, Ignatius of Loyola, who posed the sacramental principle as 'to see God in all things'; we hear an echo, too, of the poetic lines of another brother Jesuit that 'the world is charged with the grandeur of God. It will flame out, like shining from shook foil' (Gerard Manley Hopkins, *Poems and Prose*, 27).
3. *Nostra Aetate* 1, in Walter M. Abbott (ed.), *The Documents of Vatican II*, New York 1966, 661.
4. Ibid, 2, p. 662.
5. Ibid.
6. Ibid, 663.
7. I use 'story' as a metaphor for the whole reality of Christian faith, past and present, as it takes expression in many symbolic forms. These forms include: scriptures, traditions and liturgies; creeds, dogmas, doctrines and theologies; sacraments and rituals; symbols, myths, gestures and religious language patterns; spiritualities, values, laws and expected life-styles; songs and music, dance and drama; art, artefacts and architecture; memories of holy people; the celebration of holy times and appreciation of holy places; community structures and forms of governance, and so on. For further elaboration on my use of the metaphors 'story' and 'vision' see *Sharing*

Faith: A Comprehensive Approach to Religious Education and Pastoral Ministry, San Francisco 1991, esp. Ch. 4.

8. Dogmatic Constitution on Divine Revelation 10, in Abbott, *Documents of Vatican II* (n. 3), 117.

9. Ibid, 9, p. 117.

10. Ibid, 4, p. 113.

11. Ibid, 8, p. 116.

12. Paul Ricoeur, *Interpretation Theory: Discourse and the Surplus of Meaning*, Fort Worth, Tx 1976, 91.

13. See, for example, David Tracy, *The Analogical Imagination*, New York and London 1981, 99–153.

14. Ibid, 102.

15. David Tracy, *Plurality and Ambiguity: Hermeneutics, Religion, Hope*, San Francisco and London 1987, 14.

16. Tracy, *Analogical Imagination* (n. 13), 154.

17. Hans-Georg Gadamer, *Truth and Method*, New York and London, Second, Revised Edition 1992, esp. 381–8.

18. 'Application is neither a subsequent nor a merely occasional part of the phenomenon of understanding, but codetermines it as a whole from the beginning' (ibid, 324).

19. Georgia Warnke, *Gadamer: Hermeneutics, Tradition and Reason*, Stanford 1987, 139.

20. Gadamer, *Truth and Method*, (n. 17), 309.

21. See ibid, 306–7.

22. Decree on Ecumenism 11, in Abbott, *Documents of Vatican II*, (n. 3), 354.

23. See Tracy, *Plurality and Ambiguity* (n. 15), 18–24.

24. Gadamer, *Truth and Method* (n. 17), 385.

25. Tracy, *Plurality and Ambiguity* (n. 15), 19.

26. See Jürgen Habermas, *Theory of Communicative Action*, Vol. 1, Boston 1984, esp. 285ff.

27. See Thomas H Groome, *Christian Religious Education: Sharing Our Story and Vision*, San Francisco 198;, esp. Chs. 9 and 10; *Sharing Faith: A Comprehensive Approach to Religious Education and Pastoral Ministry*, San Francisco 1991, esp. Part II.

28. For further reflections see Groome, *Sharing Faith*, 152–4.

29. Mary Boys has developed the term 'to make accessible' as a description of the task of the religious educator apropos the religious tradition. See, for example, *Educating in Faith: Maps and Visions*, San Francisco 1989, 209.

Special Column 1994/2

End of Utopia – End of History?

Since the undramatic, banal collapse of socialism in the former Eastern block in 1989/1990 one has been able to read something in any of the better newspapers about 'the end of utopia'. Both old conservatives and neo-conservatives are thus triumphing over their opponents of the Left.

In 1991 Joachim Fest, the editor of the famous German newspaper *Frankfurter Allgemeine Zeitung*, wrote a book on this new trend in Germany entitled *A Dream Destroyed. The End of the Utopian Era*. It began with the astonishing assertion that with the 'end of socialism' not only this one utopia but all utopias generally had 'died the death' and therefore people had to live 'in the future without the great tam-tam of utopias'. The 'price of modernity' is now said to be 'life without utopia'. If one asks in amazement how it can be that the death of socialism as put into practice should also be the death of utopian socialism – which was fought against by all the Marxists after Marx – one is told that not only has utopian socialism died but also democracy with its French Revolution dream of 'freedom, equality and brotherhood'. Not only this utopia or that but a whole 'utopian age' is now said to have come to an end. The French Revolution was the first solemn attempt to translate utopian ideas into political practice, and socialism was the last. 'To the degree that only the most extreme eschatological seriousness underlies them, all these dreams of a new order, whether orientated on the past or on the "goal of history", inevitably issue in terror, whatever their original impulse may have been' (p. 57).

Joachim Fest overlooked the fact that with his prophesied 'end of the utopian age' he was also announcing the death of the 'American dream' of the 'self-evident truths' that all human beings are created free and equal, as the Declaration of Independence puts it. He forgot that the 1948 Universal Declaration of Human Rights is an ideal, as the preamble said, which the

United Nations so desperately attempts to put into practice. It was composed after the experiences of inhuman dictatorships with the resolve to create a new and peaceful world order. It was the experiences of political terror which brought into life this universally recognized utopia of justice. In the same way as this utopia sets out to protect the freedom of all men and women, so the social utopias set out to protect the equality of all men and women. In the same way as those utopias of justice represent the hopes of the humiliated and hurt, so the social utopias represent the hopes of the weary and heavy-laden. Since the American and French Revolutions, the two have belonged together: there can be no equality without freedom, no freedom without equality. All human beings are born 'free and equal'. In the postwar conflict between East and West, in the end the freedom of the West proved superior to the equality of the East. But for that very reason, in the post-communist period the task will be equality in the form of social and economic justice, in and between the societies on this earth.

So who are the subjects of the visions of a free and just life? They are the oppressed people and the hungry masses. As long as these exist, there will also be utopian projects for overcoming humiliation and exploitation. As long as there is such misery there is also hope for a future which is different from the sufferings of the present. Hope is the life-force of the victims of the present systems of the world. Because they cannot have a fair share in the present they long for an alternative future. Of course specific ideas about this hope change, because they relate to the concrete experience of the misery of oppression, the death of children and the devastation of the natural basis of life. Utopias come and go, but hope remains.

Who wants an 'end of utopia', and who is served by the dark 'end of the utopian age'? The answer is obvious. Those who dominate and enjoy the present want to extend their present into the future and are afraid of any alternative future. They want to suppress the 'underside of their history' from public awareness. So they declare that their system is the 'end of history', to which, as modern cynicism has it, there is 'no alternative'.

Francis Fukuyama has become the prophet of this new political and economic apocalyptic. He is a member of the planning staff in the State Department in Washington, the spokesman of American neo-conservatives and as a later pupil of Alexandre Kojève, a right-wing Hegelian. According to his famous article 'The End of History?' in *The National Interest* 16, 1989, 3–18, the triumph of the West consists in the fact that all the great alternative systems to 'liberal democracy and global marketing', all the things like Fascism, nationalism and socialism, are exhausted. No further alternatives can be recognized. So we are at the beginning of a time without alternatives which Kojève with his arbitrary interpretation of Hegel called 'the end of history', 'posthistory'. For Fukuyama, as for all other prophets of posthistory like Cournot, de Man, Seidenberg, Gehlen and so on, this is no promise of happiness: 'The end of history will be a very sad time . . . In the posthistoric period there will be neither art nor philosophy, just the perpetual caretaking of the museum of human history.' He developed this later view in his book *The End of History* (New York 1991), in which he gave a more differentiated account. His interpretation of the age was in tune with the mood of the age. Even the sober *Herald Tribune* in 1990 broke out into eschatological jubilation: 'After some millennia of trying out various systems we are now ending this millennium in the certainty that in pluralistic capitalist democracy we have found what we were looking for. There can still be endless improvements to the system and approaches to perfection in postmodernity, but there are no longer any alternatives to the fundamentals of the system.

The notion that human history has reached its end when there are no longer any alternatives to the present political and economic system is a false conclusion which Hegel himself did not draw. All human life-systems have been and are changed when their intrinsic contradictions become intolerable. Who bears the cost for the 'global marketing' of all things? What does the world market look like from below when seen through the eyes of the millions of unemployed, with the eyes of people in the Third World, with the eyes of the nature that is being marketed? The protest of human beings who have been made superfluous and of the earth which has been raped will not leave the world in its present state. Anyone who proclaims 'the end of history' over it wills the downfall of the world, for, as Erich Fried remarked, 'anyone who wants the world to remain as it is does not want it to remain'. If this world is to survive, we need utopian visions which lead people out of the misery they are experiencing. 'Where there is no vision, the people perish.' Their creative source is the unconditional Yes which is spoken by the hope of life. The hope for the kingdom of God and God's righteousness which Christian faith arouses and keeps alive is a great affirmation of life.

Jürgen Moltmann

The editors of the Special Column are Norbert Greinacher and Bas van Iersel. The content of the Special Column does not necessarily reflect the views of the Editorial Board of Concilium.

Contributors

SILVIA SCHROER was born in Münster, Westphalia, in 1958. She studied ancient philology and Catholic theology in Münster, Munich and Fribourg, gaining her doctorate in 1986 with 'In Israel gab es Bilder', OBO 74, Fribourg and Göttingen 1987. She gained her Habilitation in 1989 with an iconographic study of two goddess motives on seal stamps from Palestine/Israel (published in O. Keel, H. Keel-Leu and S. Schroer, *Studien zu den Stempelsiegeln aus Palästina/Israel II*, OBO 88, Fribourg and Göttingen 1991. She has taught for a number of years as head of the Pastoral Bible Centre of the Swiss Catholic Bible Society in Zurich, and has also been visiting lecturer in both Catholic and Protestant German-speaking faculties. She has written a good deal on ancient Near Eastern iconography, Old Testament, and feminist critical Bible reading. At present she is collaborating in a research project on Palestinian pictorial art.

Address: Zwyssigstrasse 2, CH 6006 Lucerne, Switzerland.

ROBERT SCHREITER was born in 1947 in the USA. He studied psychology and philosophy at St Joseph's College in Indiana, and theology at the Catholic University of Nijmegen, the Netherlands, where he received his doctorate in 1974. He was ordained a priest in the Society of the Precious Blood (C. PP. S.) in 1975. Since 1974 he has taught at the Catholic Theological Union in Chicago, where he is now a professor of doctrinal theology. He has published six books, including *Constructing Local Theologies* (1985) and *Reconciliation* (1992). He is the general editor of the Faith and Cultures series for Orbis Books, and serves in editorial advisory capacities for several journals, including *Concilium*.

Address: 5401 South Cornell Avenue, Chicago, IL 60615 USA.

GIANCARLO COLLET was born in 1945, the child of Italian migrant labourers, in Brunnen, Switzerland. A lay theologian, he studied philosophy and theology in Lucerne and gained his doctorate in theology in Tübingen. After working for a long time in Mexico he became Professor of Mission in the Catholic Faculty of the University of Münster. His major work is *Das Missionsverständnis der Kirche in der gegenwärtigen Diskussion*, Mainz 1984; he has also edited two books, *Der Christus der Armen. Das Christuszeugnis der lateinamerikanischen Befreiungstheologen*, Freiburg, Basel and Vienna 1988, and *Theologien der Dritten Welt. EATWOT als Herausforderung westlicher Theologie und Kirche*, Immensee 1990. He has written a number of articles on mission in journals, collections and lexica.

Address: am Wittkamp 4, 48351 Everswinkel, Germany.

MAURICE ASSAD is at present Associate General Secretary and Director of the Communication Department of the Middle East Council of Churches. He studied at Columbia University, New York, and gained a doctorate in education there in 1970. He speaks and writes Arabic, English and French, has occupied many positions as lecturer and secretary/director at various Coptic universities, and was one of the founders of EATWOT. He is married, with one child. He has edited *The Contribution of Middle East Churches in Education*, Cairo 1987 (in Arabic), and *Tradition and Renewal in Orthodox Education*, Cairo 1976 (in English), and has contributed an article on 'Coptic Monasticism' to *Koptisches Christentum. Die Orthodoxen Kirchen Ägyptens und Äthiopiens*, ed. Paul Verghese, Stuttgart 1973. His book *Shaping the Coptic Identity* is in preparation.

Address: 98 Osman ibn Affan Street, Trumph, Heliopolis, PO Box 2238 Horeya, Heliopolis, Cairo, Egypt.

F. KABASELE LUMBALA is an African priest, theologian and liturgist. He is professor of catechetics and liturgy in several colleges in Zaire and Europe, and his books include *Alliances avec le Christ en Afrique*, Athens 1987; *Ntendeleelu mujidila* (Sacred Liturgy), Kananga 1990; *Symbolique bantu et symbolique chrétienne*, Kinshasa 1991. He has also written numerous articles on the inculturation of Christian rites in Africa.

Address: 3 Pirgotelous, 11635 Athens, Greece.

MARIAM FRANCIS has been a staff member at the Pastoral Institute of Multan since 1979. She is a teacher, since 1991 a member of EATWOT, and active in Christian-Muslim dialogue and women's issues.

Address: Pastoral Institute, PO Box 288, Multan 60000, Pakistan.

FERNANDO CASTILLO was born in Santiago, Chile, in 1943. He studied philosophy, sociology and theology in Santiago, Münster and Sussex. He holds a doctorate in theology and has lectured at the universities of Santiago, Münster and Fribourg. He is currently engaged on research at the Diego de Medellin Ecumenical Centre in Santiago. His major publications are *Theologie aus der Praxis des Volkes* (1978), *La Iglesia de los pobres en América Latina* (1983) and *Iglesia liberadora y Politica* (1986).

Address: Casilla 386–V, Correo 21, Santiago 21, Chile.

JEAN-GUY NADEAU was born in Montreal in 1950. He studied philosophy at St Paul University, Ottawa, and gained a doctorate in theology at the University of Montreal, where he teaches moral theology, practical theology and pastoral praxeology. He has written *La prostitution, une affaire de sens. Étude de pratiques sociales et pastorales*, 1987, and edited *La praxéologie pastorale*, 1987, and *L'interprétation, un défi de l'action pastorale*, 1989. He has also written a number of articles on pastoral praxeology, prostitution and suffering.

Address: 2637 de Soissons, Montreal, Quebec H3S 1V8, Canada.

GREGORY BAUM was born in Berlin in 1923; since 1940 he has lived in Canada. He studied at McMaster University in Hamilton, Ontario; Ohio State University; the University of Fribourg, Switzerland; and the new School for Social Research in New York. He is Master of Arts and Doctor of Theology and is now Professor of Theology and Social Ethics at McGill University, Montreal. He is editor of *The Ecumenist*. His publications include *Religion and Alienation* (1975); *The Social Imperative* (1978); *Catholics and Canadian Socialism* (1980) *The Priority of Labor* (1982); *Ethics and Economics* (1984); and *Theology and Society* (1987).

Address: McGill University, 3520 University Street, Montreal, PQ., H3A 247, Canada.

PAULO SUESS was born in Cologne in 1938 and became a priest in 1964. He studied at the universities of Munich, Louvain and Münster, where he gained his doctorate, and then worked from 1966 to 1974 as a pastor in the Amazon region of Brazil. In 1977 he became Professor of Theology in Manaus and in 1979 was elected National Secretary of the Indios Mission Council (Conselho Indigenista Missionário, CIMI) attached to the

Conference of Bishops. At the same time he served as a theological adviser. Since 1988 he has been head of postgraduate studies in mission in the Catholic Theological Faculty of Sao Paulo. His publications include: *Volkskatholizismus in Brasilien*, Mainz 1978; *Cálice e cuia. Crônicas de pastoral e política indigenista*, Petrópolis 1985; *A causa indigena na caminhada e a proposta do Cimi: 1972–1989*, Petrópolis 1989; *La nueva evangelización. Desafíos históricos y pautas culturales*, Quito 1991; *A conquista espiritual da América Espanhola. 200 documentos – Século XVI*, Petrópolis 1992.

Address: Caixa Postal 46–023. CEP: 04046–970 São Paulo/SP, Brazil.

THOMAS H. GROOME read theology and philosophy at St Patrick's Seminary, Carlow, Ireland and religious education at Fordham University, New York; he gained his doctorate in Theology and Education from Union Theological Seminary and Columbia University, New York. He is now Professor of Theology and Religious Education at Boston College, where he has taught for eighteen years. His publications include *Christian Religious Education: Sharing Our Story and Vision*, San Francisco 1980; *Sharing Faith: A Comprehensive Approach to Religious Education and Pastoral Ministry*, San Francisco 1991; and *Language for a Catholic Church*, Kansas City 1991. He is also author of two religion curricula for children, entitled *God with Us*, New York 1984, and *Coming to Faith*, New York 1990.

Address: Institute of Religious Education and Pastoral Ministry, Boston College, 31 Lawrence Avenue, Chestnut Hill, Mass. 02167, USA.

Concilium

Issues of *Concilium* to be published in 1994

1994/1: Violence against Women

Edited by Elisabeth Schüssler Fiorenza and M. Shawn Copeland

This issue aims not only to raise church consciousness about the existence of widespread violence against women but also to explore its significance for a feminist rearticulation of Christian theology. Accounts of women's experiences of violence are followed by discussions of cultural identity values, including the pornographic exploitation of women; a third part discusses the church's encouragement of violence against women and the issue ends with new means of feminine empowerment.

03024 2   February

1994/2: Christianity and Culture: A Mutual Enrichment

Edited by Norbert Greinacher and Norbert Mette

This issue explores that point in the relationship between Christianity and cultures where a culture discloses new dimensions of the gospel as well as being the object of criticism in the light of the gospel, a process known as 'inculturation'. Part One examines fundamental aspects of inculturation, Part Two looks at test cases (in Coptic Christianity, Zaire, Pakistan, Latin America and Canada) and Part Three reflects thinking on inculturation.

03025 0   April

1994/3   Islam: A Challenge for Christianity

Edited by Hans Küng and Jürgen Moltmann

The first section describes experiences of Islam in Africa, Central Asia, Indonesia, Pakistan and Europe and the second the threat felt by Christians from Islam and by Muslims from Christianity. The final section explores the challenges posed by Islam; monotheism, the unity of religion and politics, Islamic views of human rights and the position Islam occupies as a religion coming into being after Christianity and Judaism.

03026 9   June

1994/4: Mysticism and the Institutional Crisis

Edited by Christian Duquoc and Gustavo Gutiérrez

The decline in mainstream church membership suggests that a less institutional and more mystical approach to religion is called for, and that this is an approach which the churches should encourage. This issue looks at mystical movements in various parts of the globe, from Latin America through Africa to Asia, and asks how they can become less marginalized than they have been in the past.

03022 7   August

1994/5: Catholic Identity

Edited by James Provost and Knut Walf

How is an institution, a movement, a social teaching, or even an individual 'Catholic' today? The question has many applications, in terms of identity, discipline, teaching and so on. This issue explores its ramifications with relation to particular theological and canonical issues.

03028 5   October

1994/6: Why Theology?

Edited by Werner Jeanrond and Claude Jeffré

This issue surveys the programme, methods and audience for theology today, at a time when its status as an academic discipline is no longer possible, and in many contexts it cannot be engaged in without interference from state and church authorities.

03029 3   December

Titles for Issues to be Published in 1995

Back Issues of *Concilium* still available

All listed issues are available at £6.95 each. Add 10% of value for postage.
**US, Canadian and Philippian subscribers contact: Orbis Books, Shipping Dept.,
Maryknoll, NY 10545 USA**
Special rates are sometimes available for large orders. Please write for details.

1965

1	Dogma ed. Schillebeeckx: *The very first issue*
2	Liturgy On the Vatican Constitution: *Jungmann and Gelineau*
3	Pastoral ed. Rahner: *The first issue on this topic*
4	Ecumenism: *Küng on charismatic structure, Baum on other churches*
5	Moral Theology: *Its nature: law, decalogue, birth control*
6	Church and World: *Metz, von Balthasar, Rahner on ideology*
7	Church History: *Early church, Constance, Trent, religious freedom*
8	Canon Law: *Conferences and Collegiality*
9	Spirituality: *Murray Rogers, von Balthasar: East and West*
10	Scripture Inspiration and Authority; *R.E. Murphy, Bruce Vawter*

1966

11	Dogma Christology: *Congar, Schoonenberg, Vorgrimler*
12	Liturgy: *The liturgical assembly, new church music*
13	Pastoral Mission after Vatican 2
14	Ecumenism: *Getting to know the other churches*
15	Moral Theology Religious Freedom: *Roland Bainton, Yves Congar*
16	Church and World Christian Faith v. Atheism: *Moltmann, Ricoeur*
17	Church History: *Jansenism, Luther, Gregorian Reform*
18	Religious Freedom In Judaism, Hinduism, Spain, Africa
19	Religionless Christianity? *Bernard Cooke, Duquoc, Geffre*
20	Bible and Tradition: *Blenkinsopp, Fitzmeyer, P. Grelot*

1967

21	Revelation and Dogma: *A reconsideration*
23	Atheism and Indifference: *Includes two Rahner articles*
24	Debate on the Sacraments: *Thurian, Kasper, Ratzinger, Meyendorff*
25	Morality, Progress and History: *Can the moral law develop?*
26	Evolution: *Harvey Cox, Ellul, Rahner, Eric Mascall*
27	Church History: *Sherwin-White and Oberman; enlightenment*
28	Canon Law - Theology and Renewal: *Hopes for the new Canon Law*
29	Spirituality and Politics: *Balthasar; J.A.T. Robinson discussed*
30	The Value of the OT: *John McKenzie, Munoz Iglesias, Coppens*

1968

31	Man, World and Sacrament: *Congar, J.J.Hughes on Anglican orders*
32	Death and Burial: *Theology and Liturgy*
33	Preaching the Word of God: *Congar, Rahner on demythologizing*
34	Apostolic by Succession? *Issues in ministry*
35	The Church and Social Morality: *Major article by Garaudy*
36	Faith and Politics: *Metz, Schillebeeckx, Leslie Dewart*
37	Prophecy: *Francis of Assisi, Ignatius of Loyola, Wesley, Newman*
38	Order and the Sacraments: *Confirmation, marriage, bishops*

Please send orders and remittances to:
SCM Press Ltd, 26-30 Tottenham Road, London N1 4BZ

Concilium Subscription Information - outside North America

Individual Annual Subscription (six issues): £30.00

Institution Annual Subscription (six issues): £40.00

Airmail subscriptions: add £10.00

Individual issues: £8.95 each

New subscribers please return this form:
for a two-year subscription, double the appropriate rate

(for individuals)   £30.00   (1/2 years)   . . . .

(for institutions)   £40.00   (1/2 years)   . . . .

Airmail postage
outside Europe +£10.00   (1/2 years)   . . . .

Total . . . .

I wish to subscribe for one/two years as an individual/institution
(delete as appropriate)

Name/Institution . . . .

Address . . . .

. . . .

. . . .

I enclose a cheque for . . . . payable to SCM Press Ltd

Please charge my Access/Visa/Mastercard no. . . . .

Signature . . . . .Expiry Date . . . .

Please return this form to:
SCM PRESS LTD 26-30 Tottenham Road, London N1 4BZ

CONCILIUM

The Theological Journal of the 1990s

Now available from Orbis Books

Founded in 1965 and published six times a year, *Concilium* is a world-wide journal of theology. Its editors and essayists encompass a veritable 'who's who' of theological scholars. Not only the greatest names in Catholic theology, but exciting new voices from every part of the world, have written for this unique journal.

Concilium exists to promote theological discussion in the spirit of Vatican II, out of which it was born. It is a catholic journal in the widest sense: rooted firmly in the Catholic heritage, open to other Christian traditions and the world's faiths. Each issue of *Concilium* focusses on a theme of crucial importance and the widest possible concern for our time. With contributions from Asia, Africa, North and South America, and Europe, *Concilium* truly reflects the multiple facets of the world church.

Now available from Orbis Books, *Concilium* will continue to focus theological debate and to challenge scholars and students alike.